A Community-
Based Approach
to the Reduction
of Sexual
Reoffending

of related interest

A Treatment Manual for Adolescents Displaying Harmful Sexual Behaviour
Change for Good
Eamon McCrory
Foreword by Jon Brown
ISBN 978 1 84905 146 0

Restorative Justice
How it Works
Marian Liebman
ISBN 978 1 84310 074 4

The Pocket Guide to Restorative Justice
Pete Wallis and Barbara Tudor
ISBN 978 1 84310 629 6

A Practitioners' Tool for the Assessment of Adults who Sexually Abuse Children
Jeff Fowler
ISBN 978 1 84310 639 5

Counselling Adult Survivors of Child Sexual Abuse
3rd edition
Christiane Sanderson
ISBN 978 1 84310 335 6

Sexual Offending and Mental Health
Multidisciplinary Management in the Community
Edited by Julia Houston and Sarah Galloway
Foreword by Dawn Fisher
ISBN 978 1 84310 550 3
Forensic Focus series

Managing Men Who Sexually Abuse
David Briggs and Roger Kennington
ISBN 978 1 85302 807 6

Managing Sex Offender Risk
Edited by Hazel Kemshall and Gill McIvor
ISBN 978 1 84310 197 0
Research Highlights in Social Work series

A Community-Based Approach to the Reduction of Sexual Reoffending

Circles of Support and Accountability

Stephen Hanvey, Terry Philpot and Chris Wilson

Jessica Kingsley *Publishers*
London and Philadelphia

First published in 2011
by Jessica Kingsley Publishers
116 Pentonville Road
London N1 9JB, UK
and
400 Market Street, Suite 400
Philadelphia, PA 19106, USA

www.jkp.com

Library of Congress Cataloging in Publication Data
Hanvey, Stephen.
  A community-based approach to the reduction of sexual reoffending : circles
of support and accountability / Stephen Hanvey, Terry Philpot and Chris
Wilson.
       p. cm.
  Includes bibliographical references and index.
  ISBN 978-1-84905-198-9 (alk. paper)
  1. Sex offenders--Rehabilitation--Great Britain. 2. Sex offenders--Services
for--Great Britain. 3. Self-help groups--Great Britain. 4. Community
psychology--Great Britain. 5. Community mental health services--Great
Britain. 6. Sex crimes--Great Britain--Prevention. I. Philpot, Terry. II.
Wilson, Chris, 1957- III. Title.
  RC560.S47H37 2011
  362.196'8583--dc23
                              2011017937

British Library Cataloguing in Publication Data
A CIP catalogue record for this book is available from the British Library

ISBN 978 1 84905 198 9

Printed and bound in Great Britain

To Elizabeth
Stephen Hanvey

To Paul, for being there
Terry Philpot

To all Circles volunteers whose courageous
work tries to ensure there are no more victims
Chris Wilson

Contents

Acknowledgements

This book would never have been as good as the authors hope it will prove to be without the four core members and four volunteers who allowed Terry Philpot to interview them. The first group, of necessity, remain pseudonymous, and two volunteers – 'Geeta Patel' and 'Elizabeth Cowie' – also wished to choose pseudonyms for themselves. (The names of other people have also been changed.)

We wish to thank all interviewees. Few people warm to the prospect of an interview – even with the assurance of anonymity if they wish – and for people like those here, given what they were being asked to discuss, it cannot have felt easy. (In fact, for two of them – one a volunteer and the other a core member – it explicitly was not.) For the core members this would have been especially so. Having spoken to them, Terry Philpot is all the more grateful for their honesty, openness and reflection.

The authors hope that the core members will understand that telling their stories may assist others in similar circumstances and that the volunteers, in a way, speak for all their fellow volunteers and may encourage others to come forward. The stories of both groups go a long way to exploding the myths and stereotypes about those who offend.

Terry Philpot also wishes to thank a family trust that provided the necessary funding for him to have time to write his chapters for the book and to conduct the interviews. He is grateful to Circles UK for meeting his expenses to do the latter.

The authors wish to thank Juliet Ennis (North Wales), Annabel Francis (East), Margaret Hamilton (Wessex), Ron Macrae (Hampshire and Thames Valley), Margaret O'Brien (Cumbria) and Blair Parrott (Lucy Faithfull Foundation), the regional Circles co-ordinators, for initially making contact with both volunteers and core members and securing their agreement to take part.

Marie Etchels was truly indispensible in transcribing the eight, lengthy interviews. Her many hours before the recording device and in front of the computer screen picked up every hesitation, pause, laugh, idiosyncratic expression and linguistic habit.

Robert Philpot kindly and meticulously read Chapters 2 and 7, bringing a keen eye to errors and infelicities of style, as well as drawing its author's attention to the role of Syd Rapson, the former MP, in the Paulsgrove disturbances referred to in Chapter 7. Rachel Downey also kindly read Chapter 7 with a keen eye and offered helpful comments. Kate Wilson kindly read and commented on Chapters 1, 3 and 6. Robert Curnow provided the same invaluable service for Chapter 4. Roger Kennington, senior chief probation officer and project co-ordinator, National Probation Service Northumbria, made a contribution to an earlier version of Chapter 2.

Thanks are also due to the staff of the NSPCC Library in London who unfailingly answered every question asked by, and found every reference sought by, Terry Philpot in the research for his two chapters, and, on occasion, gave him a desk to allow him to follow up these. Their help reveals again what a superb (and free) resource the NSPCC makes available to researchers and writers.

The authors wish to thank Margaret Carey and her fellow trustees of Circles UK for their initial support for and continuing interest in the book. In particular Dr Birgit Völlm, chair of Circles UK's Evaluation and Research Group, has also provided some invaluable reflection and assistance in the development of the book.

It goes without saying that none of the above is responsible for any errors of fact or interpretation. They rest with the authors alone.

A note on terminology

We have avoided using the terms 'paedophile' or 'paedophilia' as these are far too loosely employed, even by some professionals, as synonyms for child sex offender and so contribute to the idea that men who sexually abuse children are an homogenous group.[1] We have largely used the words 'offenders' and 'sex offenders' as synonyms for 'child sex offenders', but have sometimes referred to 'men convicted of child sex offences' or (where appropriate) 'ex-offenders'. The men involved in Circles, like many others who have served a sentence and not been reconvicted of further offences, are ex-offenders, men who have been convicted in the past of sexual offences. In the context of explaining the actual work of Circles we have sometimes referred to 'core members' as those formerly convicted of crimes are known.

Most child sexual abuse is perpetrated by men against girls. For ease of reading, we have referred to victims as 'she' unless specifically referring to a male victim, and to perpetrators as 'he' because we make no reference to women who abuse (see Endnote 2 on page 186).

Introduction

Between August and December 2010, when the writing of this book took place, 11 Circles came into being. This was not unusual – Circles, still less than a decade old, is the fastest-growing approach to the management of sex offenders in the community.

The first Circle was set up in Guildford in 2001, followed by one in Reading, under the aegis of the Lucy Faithfull Foundation, and another in Oxford the following year. By 2007 there were 32 Circles, rising to 48 (2008), and 60 (2009), and by the end of January 2011 there were 64 Circles in operation. But because Circles have a finite life we also estimate that since 2002 there have been over 160 Circles in operation up to the end of that same period.

Circles have a history of crossing international boundaries. The first Circle began in 1994 in Hamilton, Ontario, Canada, when members of a local church gathered around a just-released offender. In due course, the idea was taken up by the Mennonite Church, who gave it structure and provided liaison. It was then imported into England by the Quakers, the Religious Society of Friends (see Chapter 1). The work of Circles has become well established in England and Wales, and there will be Circles operating in Scotland in 2011, volunteer training having started in January of that year. This growth is so much so that Circles UK, established in 2007 as the development, co-ordinating and validating body, has been offering consultancy in the Netherlands and Belgium, countries now actively involved in setting up their own Circles, while expressions of interest have also come from Spain, Latvia, South Africa and Australia.

What accounts for this rapid growth in England and Wales and the widespread attraction in Europe and far beyond? It is probably that Circles have two functions, summed up in the full title – Circles of Support and Accountability. Circles are primarily here to reduce reoffending – 'No more victims', as the motto says – but they cannot do that without offering support to those who have offended. Treatment programmes are now fairly well available (if not enough) in both prison and the community (see Chapter 2), but men – and this book is concerned with men, as the vast majority of those convicted of sexual offences[2] – leave prison, which has often become for them a safe place, a place that is familiar, with its routines, and where they know people and people are known to them. They may well have been in prison for many years, which makes their adjustment all the more difficult. Even the rise in the cost of a bus fare may prove to be a small, initial cultural shock, a portent of things to come, as one interviewee explains in his story here.

But these men are not just ex-prisoners, difficult as that may be; they are also former sex offenders, probably the most despised group in society, pariahs even among their fellow prisoners. They may well be burdened with the (often horrific) crimes they have committed and they may live in fear of that past being exposed while they seek the ordinary things in life, like a job and a home. What they have done may well mean that they are estranged from friends and family: they may have no idea where their wives or children live or, if they do and according to the nature of their offence, the conditions of their licence may preclude them from even entering the town where their children live. But they may feel, anyway, that what they have done gives them no right to such contact and even if contact were allowed, they voluntarily exile themselves from others.

This is where Circles come in. Each Circle is a small group – maybe no more than four or five – of very diverse people. They will have different social backgrounds; they are men and women; they may be grandparents or not even yet in a steady relationship. They may be not long out of university or have several years of retirement behind them. What they do have in common is a wish to help others – in this case, a despised and marginal group – but also a desire to attempt to reduce the possibility of reoffending and ensure that the core member (as the former offender is known within the Circle) is helped to manage his behaviour, that he is held accountable for what he does and, in extreme cases, where behaviour becomes problematic, that the probation service and the police are involved.

Both organisations receive regular communication and information from the Circle and the probation officer often attends the initial Circle meeting if appropriate and has sometimes been invited into Circle reviews. (The Canadians and Dutch refer to the professionals as 'the outer Circle'.)

Core members come into a Circle for a variety of reasons – for companionship, for help to return to the community, but also because they want to put their offending behind them. This is not just in the sense that they believe that they have 'paid' for their crimes by whatever sentence they received, but they seek help so that offending does not recur. Because while they may be determined that that will not happen, they know that nevertheless it is a possibility. And in seeking this help, they turn to an impartial group of people, who volunteer, who do not get paid for their time and effort, who are not like probation officers who are (as the offender may see it) a part of the 'system' in which, they may feel, they can never really be at ease, whatever help it may offer.

This book is the first to look at Circles. It is not an academic study. We hope it is written in a readable style to attract not only the variety of professionals who work in the field of sex offending and child protection, as well as other professionals whose work may bring them in contact with sex offending, but also the interested lay person. While that person – like all of us – will be appalled at this kind of offending, he or she may also be curious as to why it happens and what, constructively, can be done about it.

We draw together chapters which explain the history of Circles; what is known, from evaluative studies, about their effectiveness; what is known about sex offenders; the management of offending; how Circles work in practice; and the role of the media in shaping perceptions of sex offending and offenders. These chapters are the context for the stories which four core members and four volunteers tell, often movingly, about themselves: their own backgrounds and motivations and why they were drawn to Circles, albeit for greatly different reasons.

Three years ago, Clive Stafford-Smith, the British lawyer who is founder and director of Reprieve, which works with prisoners in Guantanamo Bay and on Death Row in the United States, spoke at the annual conference in London of Human Writes, a group of volunteers which befriends Death Row prisoners. He advised his audience, 'Look around you and see which groups society despises and put yourself between them and society.'

Today there are many groups to whom that applies, but child sex offenders are probably the most despised. Circles volunteers have unknowingly followed Stafford-Smith's advice. They have done so out of compassion but also out of a desire to do something practical about crimes against children. They have shown what the ordinary person, with some training but no professional qualifications in the field, can do. And, in doing so, they are a sign of what an intelligent, practical, effective and humane approach to the management of sex offenders can be like.

Chapter 1

The Beginning of the Circle

THE HISTORY OF CIRCLES OF SUPPORT AND ACCOUNTABILITY

Chris Wilson and Stephen Hanvey

Circles of Support and Accountability have at their heart a philosophy of restorative justice. One of the central premises of restorative justice is the profound belief in the importance of healthy relationships where mutual responsibility is implicit. Individuals are not only accountable for themselves but for what they do and its effect upon others. This accountability is not just a passive responsibility but is an active dynamic which sustains the welfare and happiness of others. All people within a community are of equal importance and, therefore, an injury to one is an injury to all.

This is the starting point for Circles. Their origins are rooted in the political, economic, social and judicial practices of the indigenous populations of American, Antipodean and African cultures and are anthropologically known as healing circles. This restorative practice was essential to the survival of these native people, each person having a specific and designated role. Exclusion and retribution would have been to the detriment of all and, therefore, reparation and restoration ensured their continued existence within a context of peace and well-being.

The foundations of Circles of Support and Accountability were laid by the Canadian Mennonites, a faith-based community, who having a tradition of involvement in criminal justice issues had developed Circles as a means of promoting community reintegration based on the principles of restorative justice. This process began in 1994 when the

Reverend Harry Nigh, a minister of a Mennonite church in Hamilton, Ontario, agreed to meet with Charlie. Charlie was a person who had committed sexual offences, and had been assessed as a high risk of reoffending. He had been institutionalised as a child and had spent most of his adult life serving prison sentences for numerous sexual offences against children. Charlie's high-risk status required him to serve his full sentence without remission or parole, leaving prison without any statutory supervision, support or condition placed upon him. In Canada this is referred to as a Warrant Expiry Date (WED) and is a system based on principles of retribution rather than restoration which in truth does little to protect the public.

Wilson (Wilson *et al.* 2008, p.26) paints a descriptive picture of the world into which Charlie was to be released: 'The summer of 1994 was pretty typical for Southern Ontario – hot, hazy and humid. Children abound in neighbourhoods, wearing shorts and bathing suits as they played in turtle-shaped plastic pools and lawn sprinklers, trying to take the edge off the heat.' This description highlights the reality of trying to manage in the community those people convicted of child abuse. This is a reality that in recent years has become fraught with tensions. These tensions have developed due to an increasing awareness and concern about child sexual abuse, a concern that has embedded itself into the public's consciousness.

The evidence for this concern can be seen in any high street book shop. The endless shelves of what Moran (2010) refers to as 'misery memoirs', the titles of which give a clue as to the subject matter that lies between their covers: *The Life I Survived: My True Life Story of My Horrific Sexual Abuse at the Hands of My Real Father over a 21 year Period; Don't Tell Mummy: A True Story of Betrayal; When Daddy Comes Home; and Don't Ever Tell*. These titles and others like them demonstrate a disparity between the reality of the subject matter, that sexual abuse will, more likely than not, occur within the family, and the public's ambiguous disbelief of this fact. This disbelief is reinforced by a moral panic created by tabloid headlines perpetuating the myth that families are safe places, and that stranger danger, resulting in the abduction, rape and murder of a child, is an ever-present and growing threat. The number of child sex murders, where a child is abducted by a stranger, has remained more or less static over the past 50 years (Silverman *et al.* 2002). However, despite this fact the public's ignorance and subsequent fear creates a tension that militates against the enhancement of public protection (see Chapter 7).

The dichotomy between fact and myth further exacerbates the successful and safe release from prison of men like Charlie. Charlie had a profile of a socially isolated and lonely man with few life skills and an entrenched sexual attraction to children. Sex offender treatment had been unsuccessful due to Charlie's own inflexible and selfish refusal to accept his behaviour as harmful or wrong, and without some system of support and monitoring Charlie's release back into the community did not look good, either for Charlie or the community. The Correctional Services of Canada could offer no support because Charlie was subject to the system of Warrant Expiry Date. It was suggested that enquiries should be made through the prison and community chaplaincy regarding options for support.

The Rev Harry Nigh's church – he had previously facilitated a prison programme attended by Charlie and a small number of his own congregation – accepted Charlie into their community on the understanding that they were to hold him accountable through a relationship of support. Upon his release a moral panic flared with protests and public demonstrations. (It was a scene repeated on the Paulsgrove estate in Portsmouth, England, six years later and, like Portsmouth, the public's fear in Hamilton escalated into stone throwing and death threats.) With great courage Nigh invited the protest organisers into the church to discuss the situation and to try to find a common resolution. That dialogue resulted in the assuaging of public fear and hostility through an agreement that 'Charlie's Angels', as they became known, were there to hold Charlie accountable and to monitor his behaviour.

Later that year, following Charlie's release, another high-risk, high-profile sexual offender, Wray Budreo, was about to be released from prison into a small community north-east of Ontario. Like Charlie, he, too, had spent the majority of his adult life imprisoned for sexual offences against children and, as with Charlie, the community was thrown into a panic with the news that Wray was to live among them.

On this occasion those persons supporting Wray decided that for his own well-being and safety he needed to go to a city where he would have greater anonymity and a greater access to support services. Wray's resettlement had been watched with interest by the Rev Hugh

Kirkegaard, a community corrections chaplain. He had admired Nigh's intervention with Charlie and decided to try the same approach with Wray. The significance of this support network was that it contained a member of the sexual assault squad of the Toronto Police Service, Detective Wendy Leaver. The remaining group members were, once again, Christians, but this time recruited from an Anglican church.

It is now part of Circles' history that Leaver's involvement was initially prompted because of her appreciation that support and monitoring were important for Wray, but she herself has stated that, at first, she believed that her fellow Christian volunteers would be naïve do-gooders. So part of her motivation to be in the Circle was her belief that as a police officer with experience of managing high-risk sex offenders, only she would know the true risk Wray posed. However, once in the Circle and working with her fellow volunteers she quickly came to realise that the Circle worked because the core member felt included and part of the community. And the safety of the community was enhanced because his Circle volunteers were there for him.

The apparent successes of developing support networks in the community for both Charlie and Wray led the Mennonite Central Committee to undertake the management of what was then called the Community Reintegration Project, informally known as Circles of Support. It was not long before the project was officially named Circles of Support and Accountability in recognition that support without accountability would not be sufficient to accomplish the group's goal of 'no more victims'.

Once the project had been established with the Mennonite Central Committee, a delegation, which included the Rev Kirkegaard, made representation to seek funding from the Canadian government's Solicitor-General. Despite the fact that the government had no legal responsibility to offenders who, having served their whole sentence (WED), were no longer under official supervision, the Solicitor-General needed no convincing as to the moral responsibility incumbent upon the government in providing funding to the Mennonite Central Committee for this work. Although the amount of funding given was small, it was seen as important and would provide a starting point. Over the next 15 years Canadian Circles slowly grew across the country and has been shown to reduce sexual offending by over 70 per cent (Wilson *et al.* 2009), resulting in the Canadian government pledging $7 million worth of funding in 2009 over a four-year period.

It should be of no surprise that the Religious Society of Friends, or the Quakers, was crucial to the development and growth of Circles in the United Kingdom. The Quakers have a strong historical tradition of criminal justice reform. Their philosophy and faith have clear spiritual and theological similarities to the Mennonites in Canada and the philosophy of Circles was integral to the Quaker tradition. Five years after the creation of Charlie's Circle, Helen Drewery, assistant director of Quaker Peace and Social Witness, in London, had been made aware of and had read a number of articles about the development of Circles of Support and Accountability. Having contacted the Mennonite Central Committee for further information and received their Circles manual, she recognised not only that Circles embodied the Quaker conviction 'that there is that of God in every man', but that it had successfully developed in Canada within a similar context of moral panic as was currently being experienced in Britain.

In July 2000, eight-year-old Sarah Payne was abducted, abused and murdered by Roy Whiting, a known and registered sex offender. The *News of the World*, who were supporting Sarah's mother in her campaign for 'Sarah's Law', ran their own home-grown style of community notification. This campaign, now known infamously as 'naming and shaming', not only resulted in appalling scenes of public disorder on the Paulsgrove housing estate in the summer of 2001, but also had a significant influence on the Westminster government's decision to introduce a statutory national community notification programme in 2010 (see Chapter 7).

As had happened in Canada, representation was made to the Home Office to explore the possibility of establishing Circles in Britain. The Quakers were referred to the Dangerous Offenders Unit who had recently been involved in the resettlement arrangements for Sydney Cooke and Robert Oliver, two high-profile convicted sex offenders (see Chapter 7). These arrangements had proved to be acutely problematic because of the continued media interest in the men's release from prison and the subsequent public anger that they were to be released at all. This experience had given Home Office staff an acute awareness of the growing difficulty in safely managing the release and resettlement of high-profile child sex offenders back into the community. The Home Office agreed to explore the feasibility of Circles by inviting key representatives concerned with the policy and practice of sex offender treatment and risk management to listen and learn from colleagues involved with Circles of Support and Accountability in Canada, and this they did in June 2000.

The Home Office's willingness at this point even to engage in considering the concept of Circles was significant. First, Circles was an intervention that was based on the use of volunteers and this required revising a Home Office directive that believed it to be generally unsafe to use volunteers in work with sex offenders because of the high levels of manipulation and denial associated with this group of offenders. This attitude even extended to student and newly qualified probation staff, where policy prevented them from supervising any sex offender cases. Second, this was at a time when the Home Office was engaged in a massive logistical and financial undertaking to ensure that all interventions were to be accredited. Accreditation was to be based upon both research and evidenced-based practice and yet the only evidence available to the Home Office about the effectiveness of Circles was the Canadian four-year pilot evaluation, which was far from its future conclusions of significant reductions in rates of reoffending. It is generally assumed that any statistical validity relating to this particular group of offenders can only be drawn on data over 10–20 years. Within a context of evidence-based practice, Circles had yet to prove their worth.

However, all involved in the meeting were agreed that Circles was likely to be mutually beneficial to agencies and staff involved in the risk management of high-risk sex offenders. And while the Home Office obtained confirmation that there was a genuine and widespread professional interest in the concept, it was also clear that such an intervention would be a wholly complementary practice to support the Home Office's newly instigated Multi-Agency Public Protection Arrangements. This was to be the starting point for the Home Office's agreement to fund, over a period of three years, three separate pilot sites located geographically in Hampshire, the Thames Valley and nationally with the Lucy Faithfull Foundation.

As director of the Lucy Faithfull Foundation's Wolvercote Clinic, a residential treatment centre, Donald Findlater, together with Quaker representatives, had been instrumental in securing Home Office funding for Circles in Britain. The Home Office meeting in June 2000 had resulted in Findlater questioning the previously perceived professional wisdom that volunteers would be unsuitable to work with such a 'manipulative' group of offenders. The concept of Circles had made such an impression on him that in October of that year he flew to Canada to gather more information. It was Findlater who recognised that Circles were a practical solution to providing a network of significant others to ensure that offenders leaving the foundation's Wolvercote Clinic had a relapse prevention plan that was dynamic and meaningful, as was exampled by the character Charlie in Channel 4's drama *A Secret Life* (2007): 'An offence-free life is not something you can achieve on your own. Support from and accountability to trusted adults is the key to your success.' Although it was to be a further year before any government-funded Circle projects were piloted, Findlater returned from Canada and established the very first English Circle, in Guildford, for a former resident of the Wolvercote Clinic.

The fact that the Lucy Faithfull Foundation, as a pilot project, was successful is testament to those involved in both its implementation and its operational delivery. Unlike the other two pilot sites, the foundation did not have the luxury of established agency partnerships and individual professional working relationships. Its Circles were scattered across the country and supervised by the Foundation's therapy staff, and tried to 'preserve a stronger emphasis' on, in Findlater's view, 'the original Mennonite conception of Circles of Support and Accountability' (Nellis 2008, p.8). This attempt to preserve the original concept of Circles is best shown through the actions of Richard Foot, the Foundation's development officer for Circles. He expressed his concern over the Home Office's emphasis on embedding Circles within the structures of the statutory criminal justice agencies and resigned his post to develop an organisation called Sanctuary, designed specifically to work with sexual abuse within a faith-based context. Sanctuary is now part of the Churches Child Protection Advisory Group and it continues to promote and apply Circles as an effective intervention.

Despite the difficulty of co-ordinating the development and operation of Circles across the country from their clinic in the south-east of England, the Lucy Faithfull Foundation, as a pilot, was able to offer a different model of service delivery. Circles were a small part of the charity's remit and, therefore, they could retain a degree of autonomy, independently setting up Circles in Malta, Ireland and the Isle of Man. While they were sometimes perceived by statutory agencies as having parachuted in from the leafy suburbs of Surrey, their ability to provide a Circle for a group or agency – a church, a social services department, a local Multi-Agency Public Protection Arrangement – was as important within the overall context of Circles development as it was to the lives of those it sought to improve.

After a decade the foundation had set up 36 Circles across England and Wales which, given their logistical problems, is an outstanding achievement. The foundation has now established a Circles project in London, working in partnership with the Metropolitan Police. This project is a small, discrete operation designed specifically for British nationals who, having been convicted of a sexual offence in another country, are expelled and returned to Britain and are required to sign the sex offender register.

The Quakers had identified the Thames Valley as the area in which to establish their Circles project, and in 2002 they began to manage what was to become the most successful pilot site in the following five years. Given there existed a framework of restorative-based practice amongst both police and the probation service in the Thames Valley, this was to prove an astute strategy and played no small part in the project's success. Sir Charles Pollard, a former chief constable, had invested heavily in restorative-based policing. Thames Valley Probation had been involved in the creation of one of three national accredited sex offender treatment programmes and Tim Newell, a local resident, was a former prison governor of Grendon Underwood, the therapeutic prison. Newell had been an advocate and author on restorative justice and, as a Quaker, had been instrumental with Helen Drewery and Donald Findlater in securing government funding for the three pilot sites.

One of the authors (Chris Wilson) and Rebekah Saunders were appointed by Quaker Peace and Social Witness to develop and implement Circles in the Thames Valley. Both were experienced practitioners in the treatment and risk management of sex offenders and recognised the different cultural and statutory context in which Circles was to be implemented. Their intention was to adapt the Circles model so that they could support the statutory agencies in the successful management of high-risk sex offenders being released from prison back into the community. The fundamental difference between the Canadian and British model was to be that 'while the model for Canadian Circles is organic, the UK model is systemic' (Quaker Peace and Social Witness 2005, p.6).

The period of preparation before the creation of the project's first Circle was to pay significant dividends. Being both known and trusted by their statutory colleagues proved to be a considerable asset for Wilson and Saunders who were able to design and develop a Circle model relevant to the context of the new Multi-Agency Risk Management Arrangements. This was to include a criterion for recipients that would both complement and dovetail with the prison and community treatment programmes. Working closely with the other two pilot sites, they created a volunteer training programme that would help to elicit the attitudes and beliefs of prospective volunteers. Protocols with their statutory partners were written and signed and volunteer recruitment strategies devised and implemented.

Having spent the spring and summer of 2002 creating the theoretical framework to underpin the context in which this Circle would operate, August of that year saw the horrific abduction and murder of Jessica Chapman and Holly Wells in Soham, Cambridgeshire. The adage that 'timing is everything' appeared to have a fatalistic inevitability. Initially thinking it was over before they had started, the media's insatiable need to feed off such a terrible event resulted in the Circles office becoming a media circus. Circles' introduction to the wider public was informed through national headlines such as 'What a waste of our cash' (Kilroy-Silk 2002).

However, the media's attention on Circles highlighted an important truth that Circles afford communities the opportunity to play their part in the prevention of further sexual abuse by those people known to have committed sexual offences. Significant numbers of the people appalled by the tabloids' agenda to randomly 'name and shame' offenders transposed into a constant flow of volunteer enquiries, and by the autumn of 2002 Thames Valley Circles had run their first volunteer training event. The ability to do this was fortuitous as their first referral came shortly afterwards from an unexpected source. It was a telephone call direct from the Home Office asking whether a Circle could be provided for a high-risk predatory sex offender named Peter.

Peter had a long history of sexually abusing children, including offences of child abduction and rape. He was due to be released from prison having served a custodial sentence for the breach of a sex offender order. Such was the authorities' concern over the risk he would pose upon his release that the Home Office had been directly involved in his release plan. Peter had, of his own volition, agreed to reside at a local probation hostel and be electronically tagged. He had never had any treatment and remained in partial denial about much of his offending, and his desire to desist from further offending appeared questionable. The similarity was not lost on the project's staff that Peter, like Charlie, had the same offending profile, both had a learning disability and upon release neither was subject to any statutory supervision. The risk that Peter posed was considered so serious that a previous psychologist's report had expressed the fear that future offending could lead to the death of a child. Once again an ominous sense of foreboding descended over the project but, in truth, the expectations of both the Home Office and local statutory agencies were justified. As with Charlie eight years previously, without a system of support and monitoring, Peter's release back into the community was not favourable, either for Peter or the community.

It is important to recognise that the British system, unlike that of Canada, was able to co-ordinate a plan after release that involved relevant agencies on an offender not subject to any statutory supervision. Peter continued to be bound by the terms of his sex offender order and was required to register as a sex offender, but his agreement to be accommodated at a probation hostel and be electronically tagged was voluntary.

Approved probation hostel premises specialise in the housing and management of offenders who present a high risk of harm to the public. The Circles project was fortunate to have the support of the hostel's management and staff in ensuring the success of this Circle. It also helped to develop a 'through the gate' model of practice. This allowed Circle volunteers to develop a relationship with the offender while the offender was still subject to the boundaries and control of institutional premises. Such a model facilitates a seamless transfer from incarceration to a community of care which can provide intense support and monitoring.

Given the very high risk status of Peter, it was important that this Circle was as robust as possible and the Circle worked tirelessly in helping to facilitate access to employment while supporting his move from the probation hostel into independent accommodation. After a year of working with Peter, the Circle of volunteers was observing significant changes in his self-esteem, confidence and personal hygiene. He had begun to talk to the volunteers about his past offending, acknowledging issues that he had previously denied. However, with the growth of Peter's confidence came complacency. The Circle began to detect renewed manipulation and deviant behaviour, replicating some of the issues evident in his past offending behaviour. Further problems came to light when Circle volunteers discovered that Peter had begun to groom young girls living nearby. He was recalled immediately to the probation hostel while the police carried out further investigations. He was once again in breach of his sex offender order and faced a further charge of grooming under the newly implemented Sexual Offences Act 2003. Upon sentence the court concluded that the Circle had prevented a serious further offence taking place and sentenced Peter to a three-year probation order with a condition of residence back at the probation hostel.

The hostel's manager observed that:

> Circles of Support and Accountability had provided a valuable resource in working with some of the hostel's highest risk offenders. The Circles had supported and enhanced the risk management process of resident sex offenders by developing a supportive relationship and helping to assist their safe reintegration into the community. (Quaker Peace and Social Witness 2005, p.43)

Staff at the hostel had been so impressed by the work of Circles that two of them had undertaken Circles' training and had themselves become volunteers.

In Hampshire the project was to be a partnership between the probation service and the Hampton Trust, a local charity working predominantly with young offenders. In retrospect the project was fated from the start. Funded with a part-time post which, with hindsight, was not sufficient either to engender confidence in the idea or to provide the impetus to drive the project to success, a number of the Hampton Trust's trustees also remained ambivalent about the value of Circles. Nellis comments that Sue Wade, the then deputy chief probation officer, had 'hoped that a Hampshire pilot would demonstrate that a statutory–voluntary sector partnership could manage Circles of

Support and Accountability without the faith community dimension that the Quakers brought to it' (Nellis 2008, p.7). Core members were not referred to the project as both police and probation staff remained cynical about the idea of Circles, and the policy of resisting volunteer recruitment from faith communities resulted in only one Circle being created over two years. In comparison, the Thames Valley, during the same period, had set up 18 Circles, which led the Home Office in 2005 to increase funding and ask the Quakers to breathe new life into the Hampshire project.

During the following three years, Circles in Hampshire proved successful under Quaker management. The police were persuaded to fund a conference in June 2005 held at Portsmouth University and Detective Wendy Leaver from Canada was invited as a key speaker. Leaver was the answer to the project's prayers, not only persuading the large audience of police personnel that Circles was an effective intervention but also helping to secure the continuing financial support from Hampshire police. Hampshire probation service supported the project both strategically and financially and practitioner confidence in Circles grew. The success both in Thames Valley and Hampshire had led to the appointment of two more full-time co-ordinators and Hampshire probation service seconded a full-time member of its staff to the project. In April 2008 the Quakers relinquished their management of the project and HTV Circles, as it then became known, was launched as an independent charity.

The success of Hampshire and Thames Valley Circles has been acknowledged throughout its history. In 2004 Thames Valley Circles was awarded the Longford Award, presented to staff by Archbishop Desmond Tutu. Two years later their work was acknowledged with an award presented by the Howard League, and in 2007 they received the government's own Justice Award. This was followed in 2010 when all their volunteers were acknowledged through the Queen's Award for Volunteering. In eight years the project has set up a total of 74 Circles.

The very existence of the government-funded pilot sites appeared to ignite the imaginations of those agencies charged and concerned with public protection. The interest was immediate and, encouraged by the early evidence of effectiveness, it led to a number of police and probation areas funding their own Circle projects with the support of various charitable trusts. The speed of this development gave rise to concern, and assurance was needed that any new project would operate within the theoretical framework for best practice and to nationally applied standards of governance and service delivery. Therefore, in 2005, the Home Office commissioned the Quakers to engage in a consultation which resulted in the launching of a new independent charitable organisation in 2007, known as Circles UK. This new charity was to be an umbrella organisation for local Circle projects with six key objectives:

- *Development.* To ensure the development and delivery of Circles of Support and Accountability through the provision and co-ordination of information, advice, training and development support.

- *Quality assurance.* To ensure the quality and consistency of practices through the development and implementation of training and assessment processes for local service delivery.

- *Learning, evaluation and research.* To develop learning about Circles practice through discussion, evaluation and research.

- *Public awareness and media relations.* To promote awareness and provide consistent, accurate information about Circles within the media and through public contact.

- *Influence.* To develop and maintain the profile of Circles activity with strategic partners at national and regional level.

- *Sustainability.* To ensure the sustainability of Circles and to support their expansion into mainstream activity by adopting a co-ordinated and high-level approach to funding negotiations.

Circles UK has produced a national Code of Practice, compliance with which means all projects having to demonstrate a sustainable and solid practice base. An annual process of individual project reviews that focus on project governance and service delivery measured against the Code of Practice criteria has been introduced, and a successful outcome ensures continuing membership of the project within Circles UK. Membership entitles individual projects to the use of the trademarked logo and national brand (a form of quality kitemark) and facilitates the project's access to the various support entitlements. Through its federation, Circles UK supports a growing number of individual member projects spread across England and Wales, all of which have the backing of their local police and probation area, formalised through signed service level agreements with the relevant strategic management board. Both funding and media protocols have been written and disseminated in an effort to support and sustain local projects. Evaluation is essential in ensuring the appropriate use and allocation of resources, and as such Circles UK has developed a specific risk assessment tool known as the Dynamic Risk Review, as well as commissioning a four-year national research programme under the aegis of the University of Leeds. It is believed that data from both of these will further help to establish Circles as a credible and effective method of public protection.

As an authorised service provider, funded, in part, by the Ministry of Justice, Circles UK is also charged with the provision of national training for all staff working within Circles and provides them with regular co-ordinator forums and an annual national conference. Associate members include projects in Scotland, Holland and Belgium, of which the latter two are partners with Circles UK in an EU-funded research project funded through the EC Daphne 111 programme. Through this work, scheduled for completion in late 2011, a European handbook for the development of Circles more widely across other European states will be made available.

Circles of Support and Accountability are now recognised by professionals and public alike as a credible and sensible system of support, helping to enhance the protection of communities. The influence and achievements of the organisation were acknowledged in November 2010 when Circles UK also won the prestigious Longford Award, and again in 2011, as winner of the Social Care and Welfare category at the National Charity Awards.

Peter continues to be supported and monitored by his Circle volunteers, and both Charlie and Wray remained in their Circle until their respective deaths in 2005 and 2007. Neither of them had reoffended.

Chapter 2

A Man like Others?

WHAT WE KNOW ABOUT SEX OFFENDERS

Terry Philpot

In his novel *Ordinary Thunderstorms*, William Boyd (2009) introduces a character called Vince Turpin. He has been married several times – he refers to his 'wives' – and speaks openly and lasciviously of his liking for 'kiddies' to the book's protagonist, Adam Kindred. It is obvious that this is not mere talk and that his many liaisons seem to have been his way of providing himself with children to sexually abuse. He and Kindred have met at an eccentric 'church'-cum-soup kitchen in south London. Turpin has thinning, frizzy hair, a big head and an unsightly physical disfigurement – he is acropachydermatic, Roy's syndrome: his skin is like that of an elephant, which means that 'the skin on his face was unnaturally coarse and thick, forming heavy, exaggerated creases'. He gorges on his food. He has 'long, brown teeth'. Later in the novel he blackmails Kindred so that he will not reveal his identity to a hit man who is trailing him, although we later learn that Kindred's money is no guarantee of Turpin's silence.

Thus, neatly in fiction, is a popular and media stereotype of the child sex offender brought to life – his predatory, manipulative nature, his untrustworthiness, his being on the margins of society, while his external disfigurement symbolises the rottenness of his soul. Sex offenders are often called 'monsters' and 'beasts' in tabloid headlines: Boyd's character actually looks like one.

Of course, many of these attributes are found in offenders and there are men (see Endnote 2) who have committed the most appalling of crimes – some of which have even led to the death of their victims – for which they exhibit no remorse, no wish to change.

Yet offenders fit no stereotype. They come from all social classes. They may be fathers – and outwardly loving and caring fathers – or they may be men who have never enjoyed a fulfilling relationship with another adult. They may be professional or manual workers; gay or straight. Child sex offenders may also differ very much in character: strong or weak and ineffectual; dominating or easily intimidated; quiet or boisterous; kind or cruel; loving or hateful; quiet or outgoing; stern or warm; assertive or meek. They are men like others and the contrasts are endless and point only to the difficulty of characterising men who sexually abuse children.

But, in all of them, some emotional or psychological shortcoming or personality trait is to be found. Often, too, some fact of childhood – often physical or sexual abuse – which has influenced their later behaviour.

The number of men who tell their stories in this book is far too small to draw conclusions of this kind or offer any quantitative evidence about offenders. Nevertheless, even this small number does show some of the differences between them, not only the degrees of severity in their offences, but their backgrounds, their family circumstances, their sexuality and their present lives. However, all do share one thing – they regret what happened; they want to turn their back on offending and are determined not to offend again. This is what has brought them to Circles.

What is still surprising to many people, if we look at those offenders who do not reach the front pages, is that most sexual abuse is carried out not by strangers, perpetrators of the so-called 'stranger danger'. The offender is far more often someone whom the child knows: a family member – often the father but also uncles, older brothers, grandfathers, cousins – a friend of the family, a neighbour or others with whom the child has regular contact such as clergy or teachers. According to ChildLine (2003), 80 per cent of offenders fall into this group. As Wyre (2007) put it, 'Monsters don't get close to children, nice men do.'

The other reason for our surprise is related to this – how offenders reveal themselves to others, and how others perceive them, is very different from the person who is acting behind the assumed safety of the family front door. And even then, that nature and the offending may not be known to partners.[3] Certainly, the offender who abuses within the family is skilful at ensuring that secrets are kept, not only by covering his own tracks but by manipulating the child not to tell. The offender may be violent and cruel – although violence is not always a characteristic of the offence – but he may also be kindly and loving.

Many victims desire that a loving relationship should continue. They do not want to 'lose' their father, only that the abuse should end.

Any sex offender – within or outside the family – must usually ingratiate himself with the child, even where the outcome may be rape. But some of those outside the family need to ingratiate themselves with the family, to show that they are caring people, that they seek the child's better good, that they can be trusted. To take the most obvious, too common, example of this, some men may enter into relationships with single mothers for the purpose of gaining access to their children.

Marshall (1997) showed that, in 1993, 110,000 men aged 20 and over had convictions for a sexual offence against a child. This equated to one in 150 men, although it did not include rape. However, when rape was included the ratio rose to one in 140 men aged 20 and over.[4]

Types of child sex offender

I have referred briefly to those personality factors which motivate offenders, as well as to the differences between offenders. Mann *et al.* (2002) has identified motivations and looked at some of the differences that impact on this. They found that one factor is how sexual interest operates. Children may be the cause of arousal in some offenders, while others may turn to sexual thoughts of children in difficult situations or in difficult emotional states. Sex may be a literal obsession for some offenders or they may use sexual outlets to cope with negative moods. Some offenders may have sadistic motives and it is violent aspects of sex which arouse them.

Another factor identified was how offenders differ in their attitudes to sexual abuse. Shame at what they have done is one characteristic, but this marries with their 'giving in to temptation' when under pressure – and such pressure may be an obsession with sex. Others may never consider the child a victim and convince themselves that they are not harming her. Others may find something about the child that makes the abuse 'acceptable', even if they understand it to be wrong. A minority of abusers take the view that sexual activity with children is acceptable, that maybe the child likes it, even desires it, or deliberately provokes their actions. In such cases, of course, the concept of abuse is alien. Such offenders who were themselves abused may convince themselves that what happened to them did them no harm.

A third set of variables which Mann and colleagues found is how people relate to others. Feelings of inadequacy or problems in intimate relationships with other adults may make some offenders feel more comfortable with children. They see them as non-threatening, but they may also give the offender a sense of power or feed narcissistic desires. The desire to offend can be fed by a deep, inchoate sense of grievance against the world. Here the offender sees himself as disadvantaged by others, and feels vengefulness.

Offenders may also find it difficult to manage their emotions; emotional factors and difficult situations may provoke abusive behaviour which is otherwise kept under control.

The sex offender's sexual interests differ markedly. They may be gay or straight; they may be married or unable to make a stable (or any) relationship with another adult; young children or maturing teenagers (of either sex) may sexually arouse them; toddlers, even babies, may arouse others. They may be attracted sexually to children or only to one or two children whom they know. With these considerations in mind, we can see that it is not true that the sexual orientation of all offenders is exclusively towards children.

Offenders who are uncovered (if they are, one should add, given that most sexual offending goes undetected and the majority of those who appear in court are acquitted) may express remorse. Even then the responses hide a variety of motives. These may be an attempt to lessen the anger that others feel against him; to give others some kind of assurance that his actions will not be repeated; fearful of the consequences for himself now. It may be another exercise of deceit and manipulation. It may be genuine.

A cycle has been formulated by Finkelhor (1984) and Wolf (1984), which, they say, allows how abuse is motivated to be analysed. Finkelhor's step-by-step progress of how abuse takes place requires the following pre-conditions:

- the motivation to abuse
- overcoming internal inhibitions to abuse
- overcoming external inhibitors to abuse
- overcoming the child's possible resistance.

These steps require a number of psychological and sociological factors to be present. For example, the psychological factors include:

- arrested emotional development; the need to feel powerful and controlling; and inadequate social skills for *motivation*

- alcohol; impulse disorder; and a failure, within the family, of an inhibition on incest in *overcoming internal inhibitors*

- a mother who is absent or ill or is not close to the child; the social isolation of the family; a mother who is dominated or abused by the father; and a lack of supervision of the child to *overcome external inhibitors*

- a child who is emotionally insecure or deprived or lacks knowledge of sexual abuse; an unusual degree of trust between child and offender to *overcome the child's resistance.*

Finkelhor lists sociological factors that need to be present. These include:

- a masculine requirement to be dominant and powerful in a sexual relationship; the availability of child pornography; and a male tendency to sexualise emotional needs to *have the motivation to sexually abuse*

- social tolerance of sexual interest in children; weak criminal sanctions against offenders; an inability to identify with the needs of children; and an ideology which elevates patriarchy to *overcome internal inhibitors*

- a lack of social support; barriers to women's equality; the erosion of social networks; and a belief in the sanctity of the family to *overcome external inhibitors*

- the unavailability of sex education for children; and children being socially powerless to *overcome the child's resistance.*[5]

This means that specific and general attitudes give the offender 'permission' to abuse, or he has problems of self-management which cause him to give in to temptation even if he knows it is wrong.

Self-justification is a strong element in how an offender overcomes his inhibitions about abusing. He can convince himself that he is not hurting the child; that non-penetrative sex is not really abuse; that the child enjoys what he does; that she is to blame by, in effect, seducing him into what he did. Abusers have one essential psychological or emotional defect which allows them to act as they do: they do not possess empathy, the ability to enter into the feelings of another person.

But the wish to abuse must be allied with being psychologically prepared to abuse. Masturbation about deviant sexual fantasies can be important here. The inhibitors can be overcome, lead to the abuse and then contribute to rehearsing the abuse again and then abusing again. While the abuser may begin by masturbating about *images* of children, for some offenders it is then only a short step to translate this to the reality of an actual child. In front of the picture on the screen the abuser is not abusing, he is only imagining the abuse and picturing what he *could* do with a real child. Fantasy progresses to masturbation and orgasm, stimulus and arousal. This is what the offender would like to experience in reality. Moving from masturbation to arousal allows two roles to be fulfilled. First there is the reinforcement of the fantasy in the person's mind, which then reinforces the motivation to offend. Those fantasising in this way will imagine a victim who likes what is happening and this reinforces the overcoming of internal inhibitors.

This is known as the sexual arousal cycle described by Wolf (1984), who says that it may lead to frequent offending with many children or only one child or it may lead to less frequent offending with a small number of children.

But where is the child's – particularly the older child's – sense of self-protection in this? How do they become victims? Most children tend to be trusting of others, especially those they know who are, in their various ways, in positions of trust. Isn't a parent there to protect? Isn't a teacher there to help? Children are positive about offers of friendship; they are warm to those who are warm to them. Anyone who has anything to do with children knows they have few of the inhibitions or even suspicions that adults show towards others. They do not judge on first sight, as we so often do. Children do not have much of a guard to drop. They lack the carapace we construct in later life in relation to others.

A child (especially a younger child) may not even be clear as to what is happening, especially if the abuser masks it as a game. Some young children may be too young to know that what the offender is doing is wrong. Children abused from a young age and continuously may become habituated to what is happening – abuse becomes 'normal' – and may feel unable to resist as they get older. The child may be rewarded with sweets and the like; the abuser may say that what happens is special to them, a secret to keep. While the child's parents may be strict in what the child is allowed to do – no smoking or drinking – the abuser may appear to be much more 'fair'. The child may be aroused sexually. Children can be coerced as well as cajoled: a father may say that if what happens is revealed he will have to leave the family home and the family will break up. He (and abusers generally) may say that prison awaits them on discovery. Children may also be threatened with, or actually experience, physical violence if they resist.

Grooming is a calculated act and both child and parent can be groomed – in the latter case, a single mother into a relationship or a couple into a trusting friendship. With children, grooming is about flattering, gaining trust, making the child feel that she is special, creating opportunities to be alone with her, manipulating her into a position where she and the abuser are alone together, and then manipulating her into sexual activity, which may initially be in the form of 'innocent' games. Talking about sex, touching the child's arms and legs, cuddling, or tickling them in sexual areas may all be a preparation for what the abuser wants to do by lowering the child's resistance. The abuser may pretend that he and the child are engaging in sex education. Some children may be shown child pornography.

Eldridge (1998) refers to three cycles: the continuous, inhibited and short circuit cycles. The first is what the offender uses continuously and consistently with a new victim each time. He can do so because his behaviour lacks any kind of internal brake. He is engaged in the inhibited cycle when guilt after committing an offence, or fear of being found out, may inhibit him. This causes him to stop offending for a while but return eventually to the arousal cycle. This allows his inhibitions to loosen and he can turn to a new victim or return to the same victim. The short circuit cycle sees an offender frequently abusing the same child. He moves from fantasy and rehearsal to sexual abuse.

What are the causes of offending?

The reasons why men (again the qualification is particularly necessary here that this chapter is concerned with male offenders) abuse are varied and depend very much on the offender's childhood, family circumstances and personality. The degree to which he lacks self-esteem, his social skills and his ability to make mature relationships with adults come into play. Offenders may also seek control and wish to exert power. Anger and the need to seek revenge may also be present. They may seek those most basic of human needs, affection and intimacy, but offenders may try to acquire them (or seem to acquire them) inappropriately. Such traits show that, for some, abuse is not simply about sex: abusive sex can be a means to an end.

There are also the cultural values with which the offender was raised as a child; the models set by his father (where a father was present) and mother in their relationship; his parents' (or a parent's) attitude towards drugs, excessive alcohol and violence; his own exposure to violence, especially of a sexual kind, either in the home or, vicariously, on screen – all will influence how the child grows to view others, including, when they grow older, children.

Each offender is an individual. Each is different and different elements in each individual's life and personality interact with each other and other factors within the individual to determine how he acts. We look for determining factors in those who abuse, but as interesting, in some ways, are those men whose lives are not dissimilar – who may also have been abused as children – and do not abuse, as well as the many positive elements in the lives of others that determine not only that they do not abuse but that they reach out both to those who have been abused and those who abuse.

Indicative, rather than definite, studies are available about the incidence of abuse suffered by offenders themselves. For example, Sanderson (2004) says that 66 per cent of child sex offenders have been abused as children, but the use of lie detectors during interviews suggests that this figure might be reduced to 30 per cent. Glasser and colleagues (2001) put the percentage at 35 per cent for male abusers. The work undertaken by Walsh (no date) at the Granada Institute, Ireland, had him reckoning on between 40 and 50 per cent. Skuse (2003) says that only one in eight children who have been sexually abused goes on to abuse other children in adolescence.

Mann and Hollin (2007) undertook a study where the explanations given by 65 'child molesters' to account for their crimes were assessed. These offenders had yet to take part in any programmes to address their offending. The study found that they most commonly referred to sexual gratification, the desire to alleviate a negative emotional state or a wish to experience intimacy. However, a quarter of them did not, or could not, give any explanation for what they had done.

The effects of treatment

The first requirement for any offender entering a treatment programme is the acknowledgement that what he has done is wrong and his preparedness to participate in a programme (although conditions of a community order will make attendance for some offenders obligatory). However, assuming full responsibility and remorse for his actions will only come through treatment.

Treatment does not imply cure. There is no 'cure' for sex offending and, like the recovering alcoholic, the sex offender can relapse. However, in being helped to face what he has done, an offender can – often for the first time – experience empathy for his victim or victims; he can reflect on and understand why he did what he did, and how he came to do it. He can be helped to change, and with a determination not to reoffend (the outcome of treatment) he can be helped to alter his offending patterns and manage his behaviour and his thinking.

The aim of this kind of treatment must ultimately be to reduce offending. We can say that *good* treatment works with *some* offenders. The findings of research are that well-structured programmes which are properly targeted can reduce recidivism rates from 17 per cent to about 10 per cent, or a reduction of 40 per cent (Hanson *et al.* 2002).

Sanderson (2004) says that between a third and a half of child sex offenders can be taught to manage their sexual arousal by children and not act on it. Stuart and Baines (2004) refer to international research which suggests that 'well-designed and delivered cognitive behavioural therapy for sex offenders reduces reconvictions by some 40 per cent'. This figure is put at two-thirds by Salter (2003), who also claims that a third do not wish to change and will reoffend if in a position to do so (that is, when they are living back in the community).

Treatment usually takes place in groups and is based on cognitive behavioural therapy. It aims to help group members to understand the feelings and behaviours which led to their offending and then to learn and rehearse strategies and skills to manage their behaviour in future.

Offenders will need help to manage their sexual interest; to change attitudes which allow them to 'excuse' their offending; to help them to manage difficulties in relationships without turning to children for emotional and sexual gratification; and to help them manage difficulties in their lives such as emotional regulation, problem solving and impulsivity.

The methods used are important and there is little to suggest that therapies offering the offender an insight into his behaviour alone will have much effect. Methods which help offenders themselves analyse their problems – the so-called 'motivational interviewing' or 'Socratic questioning' – combined with exercises, like role play, which teach new skills, are important.

The suitability of the therapeutic environment is intertwined with the effectiveness of treatment. The 'cardinal virtues' of the therapist have been identified by Marshall, Barbaree and Fernandez (1999). These are warmth, empathy, 'rewardingness' (that is, the ability to reinforce positive statements and behaviours on behalf of the offender) and directness (the ability to take someone through what may be a difficult process). Walsh (no date) cites 'very strong evidence that there is a positive correlation between the client's perception of the quality of the therapeutic relationship and a positive outcome'.

Other writers have added to this list: an appropriate balance between 'support and challenge' within the group (Briggs *et al.* 1998); 'group cohesion' (Beech *et al.* 1998); and 'a curative factor' (Walsh, no date). Beech *et al.* (2001) and Marshall *et al.* (1999) have found that punitive and confrontational regimes can actually make offenders worse in relation to key variables such as empathy with victims (Kennington 2008).

Medical and drug treatments have their limitations, while surgery, including castration and brain surgery, has been shown to have a direct effect on the libido but can also cause permanent damage. Such treatment, in the long term, has led to offenders taking their own life or committing violent crime.

Medical interventions cannot deal with the non-sexual aspects of the behaviour of offenders. From a time when the discovery of the shortcomings of medical interventions gave way to a belief that 'nothing works', there is now a belief in comparatively new forms of treatment. The outcomes of these indicate that comprehensive cognitive behavioural programmes are the most likely to be effective.

Medications can, however, complement behavioural therapy programmes for a small number of sex offenders. These are 'anti-libidinal' drugs which combat the compulsive thoughts leading to hyper-arousal, which affect some offenders, and help reduce the sex drive so that they have the chance to benefit from therapy. The effects of these drugs do not continue after they stop being used and also do not affect some of the motivational aspects of offending in the long term (Kennington 2008).

In three decades, as Marshall *et al.* (2003) state, treatments have evolved from simple programmes intended to modify the behaviour of deviant sexual interest to complex and comprehensive programmes that address a broad range of issues.

The Prison Service has developed the Sex Offender Treatment Programme (SOTP), which is based on cognitive behavioural therapy, and is most likely to benefit high-risk and medium-risk offenders. It was first used in prisons in 1991 and is now also used outside of prisons. Programmes in the community, run by the probation service, which pre-date SOTP, still exist and are complementary to SOTP. All probation services in England and Wales now run accredited sex offender programmes, and they are also increasingly common in Scotland and Northern Ireland.

Participation in SOTP is intended to allow those who participate to develop the skills and appropriate attitudes to enable a personally satisfying life that does not involve reoffending. To do this means that they need to develop empathy with victims, to be more trusting of others, to have a clearer idea of how to achieve healthy intimacy, including sexual intimacy, to be able to better cope with personal problems, and to know what to do to control the distorted thinking that could provoke a return to past behaviour.

Such treatment does not lead to 'cure', something which participants have to accept. This means that they need also to recognise that reoffending may occur. It is, then, the offender's responsibility, with help from others where need be, to monitor and control his behaviour. The SOTP will have assisted this by increasing self-awareness about the way abuse works. This will allow the offender to watch out for, and avoid, those things that are likely to trigger his thoughts and offending behaviour.

The Home Office has evaluated the effects of the SOTP on child sex offenders' readiness to admit to their behaviour; the attitudes that encouraged offending; their social competence; and their knowledge of how to avoid relapse. In a study of 77 men (Beech *et al.* 1998) there was an increase in offenders admitting to their offence; attitudes which encouraged offending were reduced; and offenders were found to be less likely to deny the impact that their actions had on their victims. There was an increase in levels of social competence. Results were maintained longer after release according to the length of the treatment (160 hour programmes were compared with 80 hour ones). This was especially the case for highly deviant offenders.

However, the efficacy of treatment relies on the context in which it is given and other factors about the lives of offenders, especially on release. First, some offenders do not receive sentences long enough for them to be treated. In 2002, only 839 of the 5600 sex offenders then in prison had, in that year, completed the treatment. This was 111 fewer than the 950 planned by the government (Silverman and Wilson 2002).

Stuart and Baines (2004) have commented on the 'serious deficiencies in the number of places on appropriate treatment programmes for convicted sex offenders and a strategy to respond to this lack was seriously needed'. They continue (pp.5–6):

> While the structures, consistency and research base in prison and probation programmes were commendable achievements by any international comparisons, too many released sex offenders have received no treatment programme to reduce their risk prior to release. The numbers of community-based sex offender programmes run by the National Probation Service has risen recently to some 1,800 places per year. But as many as two-thirds of supervised sex offenders do not have access to a programme relevant to their needs because of insufficient places, inadequate length of supervision, issues of denial and suchlike.

The Criminal Justice Act 2003 provides for longer sentences for dangerous, violent and sexual offenders. This may both give greater protection to the public and allow sufficient time for treatment to take place.

However, while prison certainly protects the public by locking people up and can offer some offenders treatment, for offenders it can be a two-edged sword. It can be isolating. Separated from other prisoners for their own safety, their company is, then, that of other sex offenders. This may only encourage their fantasies. On the other hand, for some prisoners, prisons can be a safe, familiar and knowable environment that makes the return to the community something to be dreaded.

Second, this latter point is related to the worrying vacuum of help for offenders – even for those that do receive treatment – on release, and it is partly this vacuum which Circles has been created to fill.

Third, programmes end and it is then up to the offender, family members (where there is still contact) and others to help him maintain his non-offending behaviour. For example, the programme run by the Northumbria Probation area allows men to attend long term if there is a need. Kennington (2008) says that this is not always taken up and it is right to say that treatment places tend to be allocated on the basis of completions, not necessarily clinical need. It has been argued that not all people need to be in treatment forever, although some might benefit from some kind of system which involves supervision (for example, that they have a meeting once a year). Circles come to a formal end but core members are still able, if they need to, to contact volunteers.

Fourth, the effectiveness of treatment is judged on the basis of reoffending rates. But these cannot be seen separately from low detection and then low conviction rates. An offender may reoffend and not be apprehended.

Since the Wolvercote Clinic closed in 2002 neither the United Kingdom nor Ireland has residential assessment treatment facilities for child sex offenders. Attempts to relocate the clinic, with money allocated by government, have been frustrated by local media outbursts and public protests.[6] Research, however, has shown the effectiveness of these programmes (Ford and Beech 2004a, 2004b; HM Prison Service 2002).

In the past two decades there have been advances in work with sex offenders. For all the negative publicity that has shaped the attitudes of many members of the public, the emergence, in less than ten years, of Circles shows the reservoir of help that can be tapped from a diverse group of members of the public anxious to do something to benefit offenders and potential victims. There have also been advances in treatment and its availability. Effective as both Circles and SOTP – and these are but two advances – have been shown to be, so far they touch only a minority of offenders, and the continuing lack of residential facilities for treatment remains.

The scale of the problem – the numbers of children sexually abused, the low detection and conviction rates, and what happens afterward to those who are convicted – is vast. We now have a very good idea of what works and we have concrete interventions with proven positive outcomes to show that. However, these are currently only signs of what a greater emphasis on prevention and intervention in a comprehensive strategy might look like if we were determined that there really would be no more victims.

Chapter 3

Managing the Problem

WORKING WITH PEOPLE CONVICTED OF SEXUAL OFFENCES

Chris Wilson

The management of people convicted of sexual offences, as opposed to those convicted of other types of crime, has, in recent times, received a disproportionate amount of attention from both the media and, subsequently, legislators. This has resulted in a developing culture of placing severe restrictions on an individual's freedom once his sentence has been served. Sexual crime differs from some other types of criminal behaviour. It crosses all socio-economic groups and pays no regard to race or creed. Cultural and legal context may have some influence on the definition of such crime, but the misuse and manipulation of power and position to exploit another in order to achieve sexual gratification is abuse whatever the culture or context.

It is also important to recognise that the motivation to engage in sexually abusive behaviour is often different from that of other types of criminal behaviour (see Chapter 2), and the consequences for victims of such behaviour also makes this crime different. Our sexuality is core to who we are and how we perceive ourselves. Sexual abuse, and in particular child sexual abuse, not only distorts that perception but will damage a part of a person's very being. No one can predict the consequences of such a crime, for they remain specific to each individual. However, the fact remains that there will be consequences and those consequences will invariably be lifelong. It is for these reasons that it is necessary to see sexual offending as separate from other types of crime and it is for these same reasons that there is a requirement to develop a specific and specialised system of risk assessment and risk management for those who commit such crimes.

Recognition of these differences and a growing awareness as to the pervasive nature of child sexual abuse has resulted in judicial and professional agencies responding accordingly. This significance of this response can be seen with the implementation of the Criminal Justice Act 1991. Prior to this Act there was no differentiation by the state for the management of those serving a sentence for a sex offence from any other type of crime. Automatic parole for sex crime was commonplace with minimal supervision. However, this legislation placed much greater emphasis on those convicted of sexual offences to address their offending behaviour. The Act required courts to make orders for sex offender treatment as a condition of parole, and once released from prison a person who had committed a sexual offence would be closely supervised until the end of his parole. Later legislation, the Sex Offender Act 1997, created extended supervision so that a person would be able to complete a community sex offender treatment programme while under the supervision of a probation officer.

There are those who point to an incongruity with the usage of the word 'treatment' and the nature of mandated attendance on such a programme, believing it to be just another method of further punishing a person. For example, Glaser (2010, p.265) states:

> Most treatment programmes are ordered by the courts, parole boards or similar bodies as a component of a punishment regime. They represent treatment as punishment by contrast with other clinical interventions offered in the criminal justice system (e.g. medical and psychiatric care of prisoners) which represents the treatment of the punished.

Treatment programmes have developed within a rehabilitative context of the risk, need and responsivity principle. This approach to risk management requires a focus on the dynamic factors in a person's life that contribute to their offending. Treatment is well placed to identify and address these factors and, therefore, make a significant contribution to risk management. Historically, in this country, community sex offender treatment programmes have been provided by the probation service, which does add weight to the view that community sex offender treatment is just a further extension of punishment. It is, therefore, essential that those professionals responsible for the implementation of these programmes do so in a way that does not demonise or seek to deprive the person subject to treatment of his basic human rights and dignity.

In an attempt to counter the argument made by Glaser that community sex offender treatment, compared with other clinical interventions, represents punishment, Prescott and Levenson (2010, p.275) state that 'professional ethics require practitioners to respect the rights of clients regarding confidentiality, informed consent and the right to self-determination while recognising the duty to prevent harm to the client and others.'

Philosophical, ethical and ameliorative considerations rather than mere political expediency should determine legislation and policy. Within the arena of sexual offending, political priorities can result in draconian methods of offender management, as has often been the case in the majority of states in America. In 1997 this author recalls watching the journalist and former MP Matthew Parris speaking on the BBC's *Question Time* regarding the implementing of the sex offender register. He spoke on how differentiating particular groups of offenders was a dangerous path to travel. Parris was making a fundamentally important point in highlighting the potential that such legislation would reinforce sexual offenders as outcasts and different from the rest of society. Indeed, in that same year he wrote an article in *The Times* entitled 'All-party witch hunt', referring to the register as 'simply a piece of electioneering' (Parris 1997). In fact, compliance with the register over the past decade has been very successful with a rate of 97 per cent.

Parris was expressing the same concerns held by many who work in the criminal justice system. These concerns were informed by the experience of the United States of America where sex offender registration was often accompanied by extreme public-shaming techniques. Often, those convicted would be required to 'wear a scarlet "S" on the front of their clothing to denote their status as a convicted sex offender' (McAlinden 2010, p.135). Residential restriction laws have now been implemented in 30 states across the USA and have created an accommodation crisis for those people convicted of a sexual offence. In Miami, Florida, housing restrictions have created shanty towns under state highway bridges populated solely by those with sexual convictions because the laws make it impossible to secure lodging elsewhere. Courts in Texas require those convicted of sex offences to display signs on their houses and cars which read 'Danger Registered Sex Offender Lives Here'. It is important to note, therefore, that Texas, unsurprisingly, has a registration compliance rate of less than 50 per cent. Such sanctions are clearly designed to act as a deterrent and enhance public protection by notifying the community of the potential danger that lives among them, but the reality is that such sanctions only serve to feed the desire for retribution, creating a false sense of community safety that ultimately puts the community at further risk. For those persons subjected to such humiliation, the statistic relating to registration compliance tells its own story. Rather than be disgraced and demonised, they disappear, only to reappear anonymously in another state, potentially at high risk of reoffending. Transient and off the authorities' radar, such people become impossible to manage.

Having implemented the sex offender register in 1997, it was to be another year before the Westminster government succumbed to the pressure of the *News of the World*'s campaign for what is popularly referred to as 'Sarah's Law' and introduced a limited system of community notification. The Association of Chief Police Officers, the National Association of Probation Officers and the National Society of Prevention of Cruelty to Children, to name but a few, had all expressed concerns as to the wisdom of introducing broad community notification. It was the Home Secretary, John Reid, who, in 2006, despatched a Home Office envoy to America to gather information on this particularly American style of risk management. This eventually led to legislation covering England and Wales which diluted the American concept to such a point that notification in the United Kingdom was set firmly in the existing approach of selective disclosure, where people with child protection responsibilities or specific, justifiable concerns could ask the police for information. It is clear, as Thomas (2010, p.74) states, that 'the government has been far more comfortable in responding to media influences than to research and evaluation evidence where it existed.' In reality, there was to be no general public access to the sex offender register despite national headlines in the *News of the World* indicating that the battle for 'Sarah's Law' had been won.

Characterisation by some elements of the media of all sex offenders as predatory paedophiles misrepresents child sexual abuse as entirely an issue of 'stranger danger'. This has severely distorted the public's perception of child sexual abuse. In recent times this distortion has become profoundly entrenched in the public's consciousness, creating a belief that the criminal justice system is manifestly failing to protect communities and that tariffs of punishment are grossly inadequate. The impact of the media on public and indeed political perceptions of those who commit sexual offences is well described by the criminologist Professor David Wilson and the journalist and writer Jon Silverman (Silverman and Wilson 2002). This simplistic characterisation is despite the fact that over the past two decades there has been a plethora of legislation resulting in the United Kingdom having what the former Home Secretary Jacqui Smith called in 2008 'some of the strictest controls on sex offenders in the world to protect our children'.

The public's belief in the ever-increasing risk posed to their children by this apparent growth in the population of predatory sex offenders (or 'paedophiles' as the media habitually refers to them) has been further reinforced through legislators seeking to pacify the media and reinforce their own popularity by creating and implementing policy based on the perspective of the electorate, a perspective which, in turn, has been influenced by the media. This tripartite configuration of media, public opinion and legislators all feeding and informing each other has resulted in the notion that sex offenders are primarily a homogeneous group with predatory tendencies who need to be managed in a system that is resource-intensive and risk-averse and who, by nature of their crime, have forfeited all rights that the rest of the population enjoy (see Chapter 7). The reality of course is somewhat different. Jacqui Smith was right in her assertion that this country has some of the strictest controls on sex offenders: however, this country also has some of the best examples of good practice in the management of this particular population within the criminal justice system.

The management of persons convicted of a sexual offence living in the community is based upon two specific elements: the Multi-Agency Public Protection Arrangements (MAPPA) and community sex offender treatment programmes. Both elements have developed within a context of legislative and policy endeavours to reintegrate people, based on concepts of risk assessment, risk management and control. These concepts have previously been referred to as the 'risk, need and responsivity' principle of rehabilitation. MAPPA is charged with the overall management of the person, while a sex offender treatment programme is designed to mitigate the risk posed to the community by developing empathic concern for others, personal insight into the offending behaviour, strategies to avoid further offending and positive life goals. Both are mindful of a human rights framework for their practice, without which they would offer little in the way of positive modelling in responsible citizenship and offence-free living.

Prior to the 1990s the probation service had been the social work agency within the criminal justice system. Its stated values of advice, assistance and befriending underpinned the notion that the successful prevention of reoffending could be achieved through a supportive and caring relationship. The theoretical underpinning of probation practice was rooted in sociological perspectives of structuralism which, unsurprisingly, was challenged in a number of ways by the Conservative government of the time. One of these challenges was through the Criminal Justice Act 1991 which not only identified sexual offences as specific from other types of crime, but reframed the role of the probation service to protect the public from serious harm. Enforcement and public protection became the new stated values of the probation service. This piece of legislation was radical in trying to ensure proportionate sentencing and helped to encourage the development of the idea of 'What works' (McGuire 1995), where probation practice was evidence-based. This agenda was to provide the foundation for the development of the accredited probation programmes of which the community sex offender treatment programme became the most effective and successful.

Throughout the 1990s numerous legislative and policy developments superseded the Criminal Justice Act, which not only continued to reshape the role of the probation service into a more American-style correctional service but also characterised its work by 'risk aversion, enforced repositioning and blame avoidance' (Kemshall 2003, p.85). One of the positive developments of this period was the increase in inter-agency co-operation. Old professional perspectives, where probation officers viewed the police as provocateurs and agents of the state while the police viewed probation officers as Trotskyites and left-wing do-gooders, no longer prevailed.

New risk assessment tools, aimed at accurate identification for potential risk of harm, were now being jointly used across criminal justice agencies. These tools were supplemented by a new culture of co-operation between agencies and the planning of risk management, which was subsequently enshrined in law through the Criminal Justice and Courts Services Act 2000. This placed a responsibility on police and the probation service (and later prisons through the Criminal Justice Act 2003) to establish an arrangement of local partnerships between the three responsible authorities of police, probation service and prisons and a collective of other agencies who had a 'duty to co-operate'. These arrangements are known as the Multi-Agency Public Protection Arrangements and became the operational structure responsible for the management of all sexual and violent offenders being released from prison back into the community. Meeting on a regular basis, it is in this forum that all the agencies charged with assessing and managing risk collectively construct responsive risk management plans. MAPPA serves the local community and its operational work is overseen by the inter-agency strategic management. Each board is co-terminous with its police and probation area and is chaired by a senior officer from either of the two agencies. On each board sits a lay representative recruited from the community, and in 2005 the Thames Valley Circles Project set a precedent by being invited to sit as a permanent member of the Thames Valley Strategic Management Board. It is the board's responsibility to ensure the establishment of local arrangements for assessing and managing the risk of 'relevant sexual and violent offenders, and any other persons, who, by reason of offences committed by them (wherever committed) are considered by the responsible authority to be persons who may cause serious harm to the public' (Criminal Justice and Courts Services Act 2000).

The level of co-operation between agencies and resources dedicated to risk management is determined by three levels of management. These levels are designed to match resources and be responsive to the risk assessment:

- *Level 1 – ordinary risk management* where the agency responsible for the offender can manage risk without the significant involvement of other agencies. This level of management is only appropriate for offenders presenting a low or medium risk.

- *Level 2 – local inter-agency risk management* where there is active involvement of more than one agency in risk management plans, either because of a higher level of risk or because of the complexity of managing the offender. It is common for level 3 cases to be referred down to level 2 when risk of harm deflates.

- *Level 3 – Multi-Agency Public Protection Panel (MAPPP)* is for those defined as the 'critical few'. The panel is responsible for risk management and drawing together key partners who will take joint responsibility for the community management of the offender. An offender who should be referred to this level of management is defined as someone who:

  (a) is assessed under OASys (the offender assessment system) as being high or very high risk of causing serious harm; and

  (b) presents risks that can only be managed by a plan which requires close co-operation at a senior level due to the complexities of the case and/or because of the unusual resource commitments it requires; or

  (c) although not assessed as high risk or very high risk, the case is exceptional because the likelihood of media scrutiny and/ or public interest in the management of the case is very high and there is a need to ensure public confidence in the criminal justice system is sustained.

  (Home Office 2004, quoted in Wood and Kemshall 2010)

The prime concern for MAPPA is to ensure that the process of risk management will be effective in protecting the community. It is a system that is risk-averse, applying control and restrictions which have often been attached as a condition, or a set of conditions, to a supervision order, parole licence or sex offender prevention order. These conditions are wide-ranging and can severely impinge upon the freedoms of the individual, restricting who he may or may not have contact with and where he can live. There may be restrictions against using local swimming pools or leisure centres. There may be geographical exclusion zones, for example within a certain distance of a park or a school. Curfews can restrict activities and movements both day and night. The justification for such conditions is that they restrict the individual's opportunity to commit further offences, which now include behaviours prior to any sexual assault having taken place, for example the grooming of potential victims under the Sexual Offences Act 2003.

It is crucial that such restrictive conditions are specific to the individual and are matched against assessed risk factors which are both justifiable and proportionate. The professionals working within the structure of MAPPA are well aware of the paradox that risk-averse conditions which restrict an individual's freedom could well have a negative impact upon likelihood to reoffend. It is this fact that has led to many strategic management boards engaging with Circles knowing that this service offered MAPPA the ability to involve the community in monitoring the individual while allowing a risk management approach that could balance the totally restrictive nature of its work against a respect for the individual's rights and desires to improve the quality of his life.

The desire to engage in work that effectively reduces reoffending through an agenda of positive human regard is what underpins the philosophy of sex offender treatment programmes. In 1984 Finkelhor published *Child Sexual Abuse*, having developed the 'four pre-conditions', a theoretical model that is still central in today's work on sex offender treatment programmes (see pages 34–35). The simplicity of this model has, for many, facilitated a personal insight into their own offending behaviour and provided therapists with a practice framework that can effectively challenge denial and distorted thinking.

Sex offender treatment before the 1980s tended to be analytical and was provided primarily in psychiatric hospitals. The growth in society's general awareness as to the prevalence of child sexual abuse led to a new style of treatment programme that was cognitive behavioural in approach and delivered by those who were focused on child protection and incorporated a feminist perspective on male power and dominance. Finkelhor's 'four pre-conditions' and Wolf's 'Cycle of Offending' (Wolf 1984) gave structure and focus to the work of these early treatment groups which were designed to challenge denial, identify distorted thinking, enhance victim empathy and provide relapse-prevention strategies. Group facilitators would model the programme's value base through mixed gender facilitation and female leadership (see Chapter 2).

By 1993, 42 out of a total of 55 probation areas were running a community sex offender treatment programme. The Criminal Justice Act 1991 had provided the legal framework for probation areas and probation officers to engage in this specialist work, and the treatment agenda in the United Kingdom gained a momentum that was to create a growth in research and practice on an unprecedented scale. The wider political and public debate about child sexual abuse was also instrumental in the allocation of resources for this specialist work, and in 1991 the National Organisation for the Treatment of Abusers held its inaugural conference. The following year it was clear that a national systemic evaluation of community-based sex offender treatment programmes was required and the government commissioned the Sex Offender Treatment and Evaluation Project report, known as the STEP study (Beckett *et al.* 1994). The study evaluated six programmes as well as the Gracewell Clinic, the residential clinic in Birmingham and forerunner to the Lucy Faithfull Foundation's Wolvercote Clinic.

The study had several aims, such as identifying which elements of a programme were the most effective and how effectiveness could be improved as well as collecting data in relation to a long-term reconviction study. What the STEP study found was that treatment efficacy was linked to deviancy and that deviancy profiles should be linked to the amount of treatment time given, that is, dosage. Therefore, systematic assessment, both clinical and psychometric pre-treatment, was essential. This was to be important in influencing the development of the three national accredited sex offender treatment programmes at the end of the millennium. The other significant recommendation of the STEP study was the identified need for long-term maintenance groups that could support and monitor the higher-risk person once his treatment had finished. Maintenance groups were never a feature of the accredited programmes, principally because of resource implications, although Circles is one very significant way in which that particular recommendation is inadvertently addressed and indeed improved upon.

Prior to the STEP study all research in the field of sexual aggression was dominated by North America and in 1995 NOTA produced the first issue of what is now an international academic research- and practice-based publication, *The Journal of Sexual Aggression*. By this time research was having a profound effect upon the way that sex offender treatment programmes both in prisons and in the community were being provided. Denial was no longer seen simply as a risk factor but could also be perceived as an expression of shame and guilt. Challenging distorted thinking was executed in a motivational ethos, using an open and Socratic style of questioning. It was becoming clear that a respectful and therapeutic alliance was far more effective in reducing recidivist behaviours (Mann and Thornton 1998) than the old confrontational styles of intervention.

The Home Office, keen to capitalise on the growth of the concept 'What works' and the evidence-based risk need and responsivity model of rehabilitation, embarked on an enormous process of implementing accredited, manual-based programmes for all types of offending behaviour. (This idea came from the concept of McGuire (1995) of 'What works' whereby a programme would be based on a manual from which there should be no deviation.) Cognitive behavioural in approach, the most successful of these has been the sex offender treatment programmes both in prisons and in the community. The reason for this success is twofold. First, sex offender treatment has responded and adapted to new and compelling research and, second, although manual-based, it requires of those who facilitate and deliver the programme a high degree of therapeutic skill and training, over and above that required for other offending programmes. So, in 2002 the implementation of three accredited community treatment programmes began in England and Wales: the Thames Valley programme was provided across the south of England; the programme in the West Midlands covered Wales, the Midlands and London; while the Northumbria programme was provided right across the north of the country.

Although organisationally the way in which the three programmes were provided was different, the content remained the same. That content would include an offence analysis, victim empathy, life skills, relapse prevention work and new life plans. Most participants would have already undertaken a sex offender treatment programme in prison and once released their average length of attendance on a community sex offender treatment programme would be 18 months. Psychometric tests would be undertaken before and after treatment and help to measure treatment impact, informing the clinical judgement and risk assessment made after treatment. This assessment would be fed back to the MAPPA who, in turn, would base any further risk management plan on those treatment outcomes.

Circles have often been created for an individual who is leaving prison and has yet to begin that process of community sex offender treatment. When this has been the case the Circle has acted as a support during the core member's treatment programme which is invariably a very stressful and emotional process. Circles have proved effective in reinforcing the values and messages of treatment and represent the practical application to one of the principal tenets of the accredited sex offender treatment programmes, the Good Lives Model.

This model is important because it challenges the notion that those who sexually offend are essentially different from the wider population.

The model views human beings, including those convicted of sexual offences, as active and goal-seeking. Their behaviour demonstrates an attempt to meet intrinsic and natural human needs or primary goods (Ward 2003). Primary goods are experiences that reflect a state of mind that is intrinsically beneficial to all human beings and are sought for their own sake, such as creativity, autonomy, intimacy, inner peace and so on. Individuals will engage in a range of activities and strategies known as secondary goods in order to achieve the attainment of primary goods. For example, the attaining of intimacy would be achieved through the development of secondary goods such as friendship or a romantic relationship. Using the Good Lives Model, people who offend sexually do so because of their use of inappropriate means to secure the primary goods; so, for example, the attaining of intimacy would be achieved through the development of a sexual relationship with a child. The aim of treatment and Circles, therefore, is not to remove risk factors, but to identify them and equip the individual with the necessary internal (psychological) and external (social) conditions to meet his inherent human needs in appropriate and socially acceptable ways. It is important to recognise that the Good Lives Model builds upon the risk, needs and responsivity model of rehabilitation by focusing not only on risk but also on the individual's motivation to change. A Circle can then model and reinforce the internal and external conditions to ensure the core member achieves the primary goods.

The value base of those professionals working within the structures of MAPPA and sex offender treatment to deliver a service of public protection is completely congruent with the value base of Circles. There are many who regard Circles as the element of maintenance recommended by the STEP study that was never fully implemented.

However, it is evident that some differences exist between the shared values of professionals and volunteers working directly with those who have committed sexual offences, as opposed to those principles reflected in the wider scheme of sex offender management, promoted by legislators, and some of the public and press. Since its implementation the sex offender register has undoubtedly become increasingly punitive and restrictive. With every new media-driven campaign, the government has sought to appease both press and public by introducing new legislation that would strengthen the register. The continual progression of its restrictive nature has led to a number of challenges under human rights legislation. The European Court of Human Rights has heard successive test cases which have clarified that the register is not a punishment but rather an administrative tool with sanctions if there is a failure to comply. A challenge to the validity of registration for life in 2008 (applying to a person who has been sentenced to imprisonment for life or for 30 months or more) resulted in the 'High Court ruling that those on the sex offender register for life should at least have the right to appeal against the indefinite requirement to a judicial body having some oversight of the register and the circumstances of those on it' (F and Angus Aubrey Thompson v Secretary of State for Justice 2008, quoted in Thomas 2010).

The Sexual Offences Act 2003 consolidated all laws related to sexual offending, which by the new millennium had become disjointed and outdated. The Act kept all the requirements of the 1997 law intact, updating and strengthening them. The Act also introduced new powers to register those who had offended abroad. Aimed at those persons engaged in 'sex tourism', it became apparent, very quickly, that a number of this group had been orphans or children in care, who, with state sanction, were removed from this country and sent to families in the colonies. Having committed a sexual offence as an adult and served their sentence, they have been repatriated to Britain. They arrive in this country which is now alien to them, isolated, alone and without any network of support. Aware of the potential risk such a repatriation posed, the Metropolitan Police, who had ultimate responsibility for this group of British national deportees, and the charity Prisoners Abroad embarked on a partnership with the Lucy Faithfull Foundation to provide a Circle programme specifically to address these situations.

There is much to be proud of in the systems that have developed to protect our children and the public generally from those people assessed as posing a high risk of continuing harm. It is, however, the responsibility of us all to ensure that such work is carried out in a manner that is respectful and exemplifies humanity and care. Continuing legislation that toughens and tightens the freedom of individuals in the name of public protection is not always in the best interest of society as a whole. If we demonise a particular group of people, excluding them from our communities, their risk will rise and others will be hurt. These are the challenges we all face in the successful management of those who have committed sexual offences and remain a risk to the public.

Chapter 4

Within the Circle

THE REALITIES OF PRACTICE

Chris Wilson

All interventions require a rationale to justify their intention. The fundamental principle of Circles is best exemplified by Goethe, when he said, 'If you treat an individual as he is he will stay as he is, but if you treat him as if he were what he ought to be and could be, he will become what he ought to be and could be.' However, quotes from German writers alone are unlikely to persuade governments and their agencies to invest their time, commitment and finances in the work of Circles.

It was, therefore, important to ensure that all work undertaken within a Circle could be defined through a specific theoretical framework upon which best practice would be based. Such a framework needs to be able to provide the foundation whereby all volunteers acting for and on behalf of their community, through a relationship of support, can effectively hold accountable a person who is known to have committed sexually abusive behaviour. It should also provide an insight into why it is that Circles facilitates the successful reintegration of offenders back into the community.

The 'three key principles' (Saunders and Wilson 2003) were initially conceived to try to address the different legal and cultural contexts that existed between Canada, England and Wales. This was to ensure that any development of the Circles' model was relevant to the environment in which it was being developed. While it would have been naïve not to recognise such differences, it would have been equally naïve not to recognise that it is their similarities, the principles of inclusion and restoration through positive human relationships, that are intrinsic to the success and growth of Circles. It is these similarities which appear, thus far, to have allowed Circles to develop successfully, whatever the cultural context.

This theoretical framework was to become the foundation for all Circles' work in England and Wales and was to provide a continuous reference point, both for the development and provision of Circles the service, ensuring a focus on the core objective of reducing any further sexual offending by persons known to be of high risk. Using the specific headings of 'Support, Monitor and Maintain', the model was designed to address particular issues considered to be important in minimising the risk of further sexual offending and to help strengthen the process of risk management.

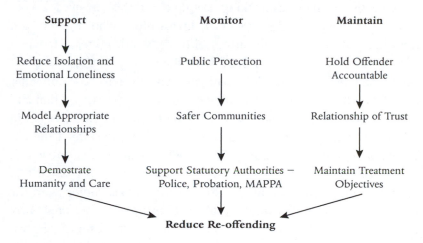

The three key principles
Source: Saunders and Wilson 2003

Successful rehabilitation and community reintegration requires support from others to enable a person to feel positive and motivated to change; in Donne's phrase, 'No man is an Island'. It is the warmth and kindness of others that affirms the positive in us all but which also guides us and holds us accountable for our actions. Isolation and rejection do nothing but reinforce the negative, perpetuating a sense of worthlessness and low self-esteem. Although such human need is instinctively recognisable, research using psychometrics (Bates *et al.* 2004) highlighted two commonalities most prevalent among reoffenders after treatment – the continued existence of high levels of isolation and emotional loneliness.

These findings proved advantageous in affirming the development of Circles in England and Wales.

It is also accepted that distorted perceptions of intimacy and significant attachment deficits are common among adults who sexually abuse children. The need for Circles' volunteers to model appropriate adult relationships is a central feature of the volunteer's role and by doing so facilitates the core member's capacity to develop a sense of well-being. In turn, this will reduce the criminogenic factors that have previously led the core member to engage in sexually abusive behaviour. It is the process of developing a group dynamic that determines the culture of each Circle, making them unique and Gestalt in character.

One of the most compelling examples of this involved a core member named John. He was a man in his fifties who had served a four-year prison sentence for incest with his two daughters. He had a high deviancy profile which fitted with the history of abuse that had been protracted and severe. John had undertaken extensive sex offender treatment which appeared to have had a profound impact on him and his desire to desist from any further offending. John's Circle began in 2003 and had been active for a period of 18 months when the co-ordinator conducted a quarterly Circle review. During this review one of the volunteers, who shared a love of theatre with John, stated that recently things had been difficult for her as she was coping with the end of a significant and meaningful relationship. She had previously disclosed this to the Circle and had found John to be a source of great support to her. The co-ordinator, alarmed at the potential consequence of such a statement, found upon further investigation that there had been no inappropriate breach of boundaries. John stated that he had 'felt privileged and a little proud that they had reached a point in their relationship when she felt she could confide in him and seek his advice' (Quaker Peace and Social Witness 2005). To this day that volunteer continues to meet with John for occasional trips to the theatre.

At some point in our lives, most, if not all, of us will struggle with a relationship, unsure as to why or what it is we are struggling with. However complex, human relationships are vital in validating who we are and what we do. It is, indeed, a rare and fortunate person who is so blessed with such an acute sense of self-awareness that they are always able to perceive how their attitudes, perceptions and actions impact and influence others. The truth is that most of us perceive ourselves as we would like to be perceived by others, rather than how others truly perceive us. For those of us who were lucky enough to have had a degree of positive role modelling during our formative years and have grown without too many deficits in our ability to engage in meaningful and positive relationships (for none of us is immune to such deficits), we have been able to develop an appropriate sense of who we are, how we relate to others and our place in the world at large. We have the ability to listen, analyse, consider, reflect and resolve. We are able to solve problems without always responding in an emotional or avoidant manner. We can resolve conflict without resorting to anger or extreme negative passivity. In short, we have been allowed to develop the ability to negotiate the complexities of adult human interaction and relationships.

Imagine, then, having few or none of these skills, finding any meaningful interaction with another adult human so difficult that the passivity and kindness you display is used to hide the anger, hatred and contempt you hold for yourself and the outside world. Consider being articulate and erudite and yet unable to read social cues. Your ability to engage with another human being remains superficial, and you lack any meaningful ability to empathise or accept the perspective of another. Envisage knowing nothing of intimacy, believing that intimacy is no more than sexual gratification and believing that the only way to achieve your objective is to do unto others before they do unto you.

It is a sad truth that these human traits are not exclusive to those who commit acts of sexual abuse but, unfortunately, for a number of people the way in which they cope with these negative attributes will lead to sexually abusive behaviour. For the individual, using such maladapted coping strategies brings, at best, a short-lived feeling of immediate gratification and, at worst, a reinforcement of previously held feelings of low self-worth, emotional loneliness and isolation. Neither brings any resolution or sustained relief from the underlying issues and subsequently another victim has been created or re-abused.

Relationships are only meaningful if they are based on the premise of honesty. It is only when there is a degree of honesty underpinning the dialogue of a relationship that there can be any true sense of trust. The core member's experience of treatment programmes will have reinforced the notion of trust combined with the therapeutic alliance as being the strongest motivational factors for change. It has been evidenced that when there is a positive collaboration between the therapist and the offender in developing goals, there results a stronger therapeutic alliance (Mann and Shingler 2006).

However, volunteers are not therapists and the Circle is not a therapy group, but the dynamic of a therapeutic alliance is replicated within a Circle. Another volunteer in John's Circle wrote, 'For John it seems to me that the most significant thing he has gained from our relationship has been the fact that it is based upon honesty. He doesn't have to hide what he has done or lie about it. The friendship is based upon openness. The use of volunteers within Circles, I think, is crucial. As volunteers we are not paid and not involved because we have to be, but because we choose to be. This changes the context of the relationships that are developed, enabling them to become real friendships rather than just professional relationships' (Quaker Peace and Social Witness 2005, p.36). He, too, continues to meet John for the occasional coffee.

These examples of volunteers working within a truly collaborative relationship are important in giving real meaning to the assertion that a Circle can support those strategies developed by the core member during treatment, to avoid reoffending. As stated by Carich *et al.* (2010, p.202), 'It is only through a relationship that defines itself within a context of humanity and care that the core member is likely to accept the relationship of being held accountable by the Circle as anything other than positive.'

The success of Circles in England and Wales was, in part, due to the strategic decision to place it within the existing structure of inter-agency co-operation. The Multi-Agency Public Protection Arrangement is the statutory structure that has a strategic and legal responsibility for the oversight of agencies responsible for the management of sexual and violent offenders living in the community. It formalises co-operation between agencies and ensures that the appropriate agencies meet together on a regular basis to prepare, take action and then review risk management plans. By definition these risk management plans will be reactive and have at their centre restrictive methods of control such as sex offender registration, sex offender prevention orders and community notification. Circles afford this process the ability to manage a specific population of offenders through positive risk management rather than relying totally on restrictive methods of control. Positive risk taking within a structured plan of risk management emphasises inclusive activities and facilitates safe, constructive reintegration. Whereas, to rely wholly upon restrictive and controlling measures reinforces a negative perception of self-worth and tends to exclude and isolate, all of which are known to exacerbate risk, not reduce it.

MAPPA and its constituent agencies are assured that 'the Circle is supervised by a professionally qualified co-ordinator who also acts as a conduit for all relevant communication and information between the Circle and those statutory agencies responsible for the core member's risk management' (Wilson *et al.* 2011). It is important to recognise that Circles are not a panacea for all sex offender risk management, but rather an added layer of support to the statutory agencies, targeted at a specific group of known people assessed as being a high risk of sexually reoffending.

A probation officer is responsible for managing people who have committed serious offences and has the power to evoke a recall of a person's licence resulting in a return to prison. However, in order to achieve the objective of safe offender management, the officer needs to be aware of the day-to-day life of the person under supervision. This can be achieved if he is part of a Circle, helping to support the objectives of any supervision and risk management plan and providing intelligence relating to any changes in dynamic or contextual risk. For the police, the weight of work generated through the management of the sex offender register often leaves many areas over-stretched and under-resourced. The ability for both the police and probation service to have a system whereby people on the register who represent the highest level of concern are supported and monitored through regular contact with trained volunteers is both a sensible and reassuring addition to the overall system of sex offender management. This was evidenced in the initial Thames Valley Circles evaluation (Bates *et al.* 2007; and see Chapter 6) which drew attention to the fact that it was the volunteers who had gathered the intelligence leading to four core members being recalled. This was important in highlighting the contribution Circles had made towards the prevention of further offences and that Circles could work effectively with statutory agencies under the auspices of Multi-Agency Public Protection Arrangements. This model of co-operation and partnership between Circles and the statutory agencies appears not to inhibit the honest communication between the core member and Circle volunteers, particularly if the volunteers are clear in articulating the need to keep all concerned fully informed.

A Circle agreement will have been signed by all Circle members prior to the start of the Circle. This will have defined the boundaries and limitations of confidentiality. It is of significance that despite this, core members continue to share problematic behaviours with their Circle volunteers, even though they know that information relating to risk will be communicated through the MAPPA process. This resonates with the earlier quotation by a volunteer in John's Circle: 'As volunteers we are not paid and not involved because we have to be, but because we choose to be. This changes the context of the relationships…' The fact that the core member is prepared to continue disclosing such information to his Circle volunteers, rather than his probation officer or offender manager, regardless of consequence, is evidence that there can be constructive community involvement relating to public protection. As Carich *et al.* (2010, p.203) observed, 'Monitoring becomes a positive and community-based activity.'

The belief displayed by various police and probation areas, that Circles provides a unique opportunity to engage with the local community in providing an enhanced service of public protection, is demonstrated through the financial and practical support they provide for their local Circle projects. One of the prerequisites for a new Circles project is to become a member of Circles UK and, thereby, gain Ministry of Justice approved status (see Chapter 1). The Circle needs to demonstrate three essential requirements: first, a project must be able to demonstrate financial sustainability; second, it must have the support of its local MAPPA and its constituent agencies; and, finally, there must be a structure of governance to which the project's operational standards are accountable. Therefore, crucial to a Circle's best practice is the support and partner work with the statutory agencies responsible for the risk management of the Circle's core member.

The structure of governance and the context in which a Circle works remains crucial to the ability of supporting the core member's objective of 'No more victims' and in guaranteeing that the objective is achieved in a context of best practice. This is realised through the existence of Circles UK – an authorised service provider, funded in part by the Ministry of Justice, with a remit, facilitated by a federation of membership to support new and existing projects. The system of membership to Circles UK ensures a quality of service in which a project's compliance can be measured against a code of practice (Version 2, Circles UK 2009). Project compliance with the code of practice follows two specific areas: governance structure and operational delivery. The code of practice defines the standards and requirements necessary as a minimum for best practice and can also be used to identify the relationship a project has with its partner agencies and how that relationship translates into service delivery. There are six identifiable standards under each heading of governance structure and operational delivery. Within each standard there is a set of requirements designed to help a project and Circle meet that standard. For example, under the heading 'Governance structure', one would find:

Standard

4.5 Recruitment, training and supervision procedures are in place to ensure volunteers are suitable, appropriately allocated and safely managed.

Requirements

  i. Volunteers have an up to date enhanced CRB check in place and are registered with the Independent Safeguarding Authority.

  ii. There is a recruitment strategy implemented and reviewed regularly to ensure diversity within Circles.

  iii. Circle volunteers receive a pre- and post-training interview and must provide two acceptable references prior to allocation of a Circle.

An example under the heading of 'Operational delivery' would be:

Standard

5.3 Procedures and guidelines are identified and implemented to ensure the safe delivery and operation of a Circles of Support and Accountability.

Requirements

  i. A Circle agreement is signed by all members of the Circle.

ii. The Circle co-ordinator is responsible for effective communication within the Circle by ensuring all members receive appropriate contact details for each other and relevant professionals.

iii. A project has a clear procedure regarding volunteer involvement with the core member once the project's involvement has ended.

iv. A project has clear procedures for a core member who has been accused, arrested or convicted of a new offence, including any recall by a statutory partner.

(Circles UK 2009)

All of the standards and requirements emanate from the theoretical framework defined by the three key principles (Saunders and Wilson 2003). For each project, compliance with all of the 12 standards and the 52 requirements contained within are tested through a rigorous process of membership renewal.

One of the great strengths of Circles is that whilst all involved share a common aim of 'No more victims', Circles also legitimately represents different things to different people. It was once reported that during one of the first sessions prior to meeting their core member, a group of volunteers was being briefed by a local police officer. The police officer, pleased to have the local community involved in supporting his role, enthusiastically stated, 'You are my ears and eyes.' The volunteers were somewhat taken aback by this statement as their motivation to volunteer, being varied and worthy, was not to be recruited as police informers! However, the statement did serve to stimulate an important discussion that focused on the element of accountability within Circles' work and the complexity of core member confidentiality.

As with all child and public protection work, the boundaries of confidentiality do not extend to protect anyone who poses a threat or imminent risk to either children or the wider public, and this is as true for those working in Circles as it is for those working both directly and indirectly within child protection, as well as for every member of the public. Personal accountability and collective responsibility are the key to healthy communities and, as such, a Circle should always be a model of these.

The motivations of those who volunteer to work in a Circle are well documented within this book. In truth, there is a continuum of motivations for those who volunteer. For all, there is a desire to make a positive difference and a belief that they, with others, can and will achieve that difference. Some volunteers are motivated by their faith, while others have a strong belief in the restorative and inclusive nature of Circles. Some have a desire to invest time and effort into a constructive approach to reduce child sexual abuse and to try and counter the negative effects of tabloid campaigns such as 'naming and shaming'. There have been a number of survivors of child sexual abuse who have volunteered their time, bringing to the work a powerful insight and understanding from the victim's perspective. Their involvement in Circles represents a powerful message that all of us can take strength from. One said, 'My gut feeling is that working in the Circle has substantially reduced the likelihood of our core member creating more victims. To me, as a survivor of sexual abuse, that is the greatest reward I can imagine – that other little girls are spared' (Quaker Peace and Social Witness 2003, p.4).

Volunteers are the essential ingredient in the success of any Circle Project and their work in Circles can be far more demanding than other types of voluntary work. It is, therefore, essential that volunteers are also supported, monitored and held accountable for the work they are undertaking. The management of their work is, and should always be, undertaken by a volunteer co-ordinator who understands the needs of the volunteers, the complexities of risk management and the overall context in which this work is managed. Experience consolidates sound judgement and it is, therefore, important to acknowledge that initially the volunteer will approach the work with a degree of naïvety. Equally, when a relationship has been established and commonalities identified, it is likely that the volunteer will begin to mitigate risk. Statements such as 'I truly believe our core member will not reoffend' should immediately give cause for concern and the co-ordinator needs to be able to recognise and process such dynamics providing guidance and advice, both formally and informally.

Volunteers are invited to attend quarterly reviews in which they can explore their experience of Circle work. The co-ordinator will also ensure that the Circle, as a whole, is regularly reviewed. If volunteers are the essential ingredient in the success of any Circle project, then the personal well-being of volunteers is paramount. Ensuring a rigorous system of assessment, designed to elicit the motivation of potential volunteers, their attitudes and beliefs relating to the work of Circles, is essential for the assured safety of all. A potential candidate will undertake a 16-hour training programme prior to selection, with continuing training provided for those who carry on as volunteers. By the time they begin their work in Circle, they will be familiar with the model and the expectations placed upon them and be able to function effectively. The aim is to ensure that each Circle has a balance of gender, age, experience and skills, reflecting a true representation of community. This both ensures a healthy robustness within the Circle and allows the volunteers to address appropriately and manage the needs of the core member.

Once a Circle begins it will function as a weekly business meeting, usually taking place in a church hall or another safe venue where a full risk assessment has been undertaken. It is at these early weekly meetings that a relationship of trust will be established, usually through the core member sharing the work he has undertaken in treatment. That work will have identified key factors that contributed towards the offending behaviour and will have ascertained future strategies and activities that can be used to address those factors.

A central feature of the volunteer's role is to support and facilitate those strategies and activities which are vital when volunteers begin individual contact with their core member, later in the Circle's life. It is also important for a volunteer to be able to recognise any recidivist-type behaviour displayed by the core member and to be aware of the coping strategies developed during the course of a treatment programme to help prevent reoffending. Many people convicted of sexual offences and assessed as high risk are, by definition, socially isolated and without a support network, other than those key professionals paid to be in their lives. Each core member will have a document, known as a New Life Plan, which is a collection of all that has been achieved in treatment and detailing these coping strategies. It is a dynamic document that needs to be shared with significant others. 'The purpose of a Circle, in its purest form, is to provide the core member with a support network, so that his or her efforts to prevent reoffending become meaningful in an attempt to sustain a balanced, self-determined lifestyle,' say Carich et al. (2010, p.203). When everyone involved with the Circle feels that the time is ready, the weekly Circle meeting will be supplemented with each volunteer undertaking individual weekly contact with the core member. Over time the weekly Circle meetings will reduce in frequency until the Circle itself moves from what is known as the transition from a formal phase one Circle, into the more informal phase two. In this way a group of volunteers can help to hold the core member accountable, and maintain treatment objectives as well as the expectations of the community and those agencies responsible for the protection of that community.

It is a popular misconception that a Circle is a short-term intervention with a life-span of 12 to 24 months. It is true that volunteers are asked for an initial commitment of 12 months and that the supervision, support and guidance of a co-ordinator last for a distinct period of time which is determined by both risk and need. It is also a stated truth that a successful Circle is one that facilitates the independence not the dependence of a core member.

However, the very nature of a Circle relies upon the development of positive and meaningful relationships. The experience of both the Canadian and their British counterparts was that having successfully achieved their objective, volunteers were often continuing to have contact with their core members once the Circle had been formally closed. It was clear that this situation had many benefits in relation to both the continued well-being of the core member and the enhancing of public protection, but a structure was needed to ensure the continued safety of all involved. It was, therefore, defined by the government's pilot projects that a Circle would remain in phase one until it was assessed as having achieved its objectives. It would then be formally closed and move into phase two. A phase two Circle continues to give informal support to a core member after an end-of-Circle report has been written and formal support from the project ceases. However, the co-ordinator will remain available to those volunteers who choose to remain in contact with the core member when needed, but will no longer attend any meetings or undertake any Circle reviews. A phase two Circle can be reinstated to phase one if concern arises or is articulated and circumstances once again demand the regular intervention and support of the Circles project.

This need occurred in John's situation. The Circle had been successful in its objective of facilitating a positive and productive role for John within his community. After they had helped him secure permanent accommodation, he engaged in both adult education courses and voluntary work in a charity shop, which eventually led to employment. He made his own group of friends and the Circle was formally closed. As time passed there was no further statutory involvement, with the need for registration and supervision having elapsed. The only people seeing him and aware of any issues related to risk were the volunteers from his Circle. Three years after the Circle had formally closed the Circles project received a call from one of John's volunteers informing them that John had begun a relationship with a woman who had young grandchildren. The police were also informed and the Circle was formally reinstated back into phase one. This allowed both the police and the Circle to work with John, initially on the specific issue of disclosure, and then subsequent joint protective work was undertaken with both John and his new partner. Such work and intervention by Circle volunteers gives real meaning to the statement by Carich *et al.* (2010, p.203) that 'monitoring becomes a positive and community based activity'.

Defining what a Circle is and what a Circle does appears at first glance to be a relatively simple task and indeed it is, if one is only giving a descriptive account relating to the objective and structure of a Circle – that it is a Circle of Support and Accountability as defined by the Circles UK code of practice, 'Where a group of trained and supervised Circles volunteers provide structured support and hold to account a core member' (Version 2, Circles UK 2009, p.6). However, as this chapter has highlighted, to define the process of a Circle, its practice and its component parts is no easy task. The dynamic of a Circle is as complex as the human condition itself, with a process that makes each individual Circle unique.

Why, then, are Circles so effective in reducing sexual offending behaviour? Because they are rooted in the principles of restoration and inclusion, they demonstrate all that is good about the human spirit. A Circle builds upon the work of treatment providers and 'seeks to enhance any treatment plan the core member may have prepared and helps to formulate personal goals which will hopefully result in the acquisition of a more satisfying and fulfilling life' (Carich *et al.* 2010, p.198). For the wider community, Circles offer an alternative to the politics of despair, offering a constructive intervention that enhances public protection.

The community is undoubtedly Circles' largest stakeholder and, as such, there has to be a broader expectation that while services such as the police, the probation service and prisons are there to help ensure good public protection, the community itself bears a responsibility to focus on restoration and inclusion rather than retribution and public disorder.

Chapter 5

The Men's Stories and the Volunteers' Stories

Terry Philpot

The core of this book consists of four interviews: the personal stories as related by four former sex offenders (pages 74–115) and four volunteers (pages 116–149). The chapters that surround them offer context to what they have to say and, we hope, allow the reader a perspective on these testimonies.

These stories could have been replicated many times over – the biographies of both parties describing what brought them to Circles and the men's account of what led them to offending – because all of these people are ordinary men and women. What differentiates them is that the members of one group have committed often horrific offences and the members of the other group have been motivated, for a variety of reasons, to support them in an attempt to ensure that such crimes are not repeated and that those who have committed them can be helped to live some kind of ordinary and offence-free life.

A Circle is an interesting and unique way of people coming together, creating, as it does, unusual relationships, tensions (which are usually creative), new understandings on the part of both parties and (as research shows) positive outcomes. As these narratives indicate, while core members and volunteers can both gain much from these relationships – and the volunteers with each other as much as with the men – both sometimes express reservations. The core members most commonly ask why strangers should bother to spend their time and energy, with no financial reward, helping someone like them; the volunteers may question whether what they are doing will have the positive effect for which they hope, given that no individual can ever completely know another person. This could not be otherwise: these are the most sensitive, revealing and deepest of encounters.

The volunteers come from a variety of backgrounds with a variety of motivations. The core members, too, come from a variety of backgrounds, but with one thing in common, apart, of course, from their offending – they wish to change; they wish to turn their backs on the past, albeit with the regrets that they express, and to make a new life, offence-free, for themselves with the assistance of their Circle.

These interviews are, of course, subjective. In the case of those with the core members, it needs to be said that each man tells his own story and offers his own view of his situation. I am unable to judge the veracity of every statement made, but, then, not even the interviewees are blessed with memories so accurate that every detail of their lives – and particularly for those whose childhoods were disturbed and chaotic – can be said to be complete or wholly reliable, something which applies to us all. Given the nature of their offences, it is not impossible that a degree of distortion may occur, but it is also worth noting that each man expresses remorse for what he did.

Each core member seeks to deal with his offences in his own way. Each has paid a legal penalty for what he did and all – with one exception at the time of the interview – had been through the Sex Offender Treatment Programme. One of the aims of the SOTP is to give an offender insight into his offences and why he came to commit them and to help him manage his behaviour and any fantasies he may entertain. It is perhaps not surprising, then, that David Dawson, the core member who had not experienced the course, appears to show less awareness of how he came to offend than do the other three interviewees.

The aim of all the interviews is, in part, to allow each person to speak unmediated and without judgement being made about what he or she says. The reader, then, must take this into account when considering what he or she is being told, especially by the core members.

The interviewees were identified by Circles co-ordinators in different parts of England and Wales, who then sought their agreement to take part. When this had been done, I wrote to each interviewee explaining the purpose of the book and the part that his or her story would play in it. I also sent a list of questions that I would wish to raise but stressed that these should be regarded as triggers for discussion and that other questions and points would naturally arise as the interview progressed.

The interviews, which were taped, took place between September and November 2010, and lasted, variously, between one and a half hours and two hours.

The transcripts were two to three times as long as the versions published here; however, nothing of any value has been excised. After they were transcribed, I (I hope!) judiciously edited them, removed repetition and did some reordering to give greater shape and sense to the narratives. The important thing, though, was to retain the voices of the interviewees, their words and the way in which they expressed themselves. To this end, too, questions and interventions by me were (mostly) omitted to add to the immediacy of what was being said. Where these have been retained they have been printed in italics in square brackets. Roman text in brackets adds a word or phrase to maintain the flow of the story.

Identifying details were also removed or changed to preserve anonymity. Interviewees were then sent the edited version to comment, add and subtract as they chose. Again, nothing of substance was changed.

THE MEN'S STORIES

Gerry Hurley: 'Prison was the best thing that ever happened to me'

Gerry Hurley, 56, was one of four brothers and three sisters (another brother and sister died at birth) and was born in west London to an Irish father and an English mother. The family were poor. He attended mass at the local Catholic church but went to a Protestant school. His parents were both violent towards him ('I just thought everyone's parents were like that') and his headmaster also seems to have been a man prone to violence against his pupils under the cloak of discipline. Gerry was abused by a priest and also by eight or nine other men from the ages of five to 13. He left school at 15, undertaking a variety of jobs, until he owned his own small business. Health problems preclude him from working now. He married when he was 18. The abuse of his oldest daughter was not disclosed until many years later and he received a ten-year prison sentence for sexually abusing and raping her when she was five until she was 17. He then tried to abuse her sister. When he was charged he left the family home. He took an overdose and was sectioned. He says he had never had any sexual interest in other children and has none now.

He served time in three prisons – in the last of which he undertook the sex offender treatment programme – and then served the rest of his sentence in Grendon Underwood Prison, a prison based on therapeutic principles. He was released on licence in 2007. He continues to see a therapist by choice. His daughters are now aged 38 and 36; both of them are married with children. He does not know where they live or where his wife lives. He is not even sure whether his wife has divorced him.

Gerry speaks fluently and appears regretful of the crimes he has committed. When we met (September 2010) his Circle had come to an end but he remained friendly with two or three of the members, particularly one of the men. His health problems cause him to live in sheltered housing in north London, where, according to him, he gets on very well with his neighbours, who, with his Circle volunteers, now seem largely to constitute his friends.

I remember my first day at secondary school [*laughs*]. I realise now this was about self-protection, but I said to somebody, 'Who's the best fighter in the second year?' And they pointed this guy out, and I went over and beat him up. And that was kind of me saying, 'There you go, leave me alone because otherwise there'll be trouble.' By that time I'd gone through years of being sexually abused and beaten. My parents were incredibly violent. My mother had a favourite trick of strangling me to the point where I would be passing out, and then she'd beat me awake again. My father would hit me as though he was hitting another man – I mean, I would literally leave the floor and hit the wall, and then that'd be followed up by a boot. I had cracked ribs at an early age. That went on really for as long as I can remember: I just thought everybody's parents were like that, I never questioned it. My friends were aware that I was being beaten up at home.

During that period, one of the reasons I think the sexual abuse really kicked off was when I was being abused when I was an altar boy. There was this priest sitting next to me on one of the pews at the side of the altar and he put his hand between my legs and kind of rubbed it. I had to perform oral sex on him. I went home to my dad and I didn't know what to say, I was too embarrassed to say what had gone on, so I just said: 'Dad, the priest got his willy out,' and my world exploded; my dad went absolutely berserk, 'You filthy mouth' and 'You dirty, little bastard,' and he just gave me a good kicking and told me to go up to the church and confess because of what I'd said.

[*Was there any sexual abuse at home?*] No, no, although I say that but this is only supposing – again this was something that I've thought about – my mother would clear my ears out with a hairclip, she would take forever to do it, and what I think she was actually doing was rubbing up against me. It's only something that I began to think about as an adult, so I think, yeah, there was something going on there, although at the time I was not aware of it.

But, also, I got kind of handed around: there were eight or nine people (I'm not sure whether it was nine or whether one of the guys I'd come across in a different situation). They were associated with both with the Protestant church and the Catholic church. I didn't realise I was being passed around, it was just that it seemed that every adult I met wanted to sexually abuse me. I am fairly sure the first time I was abused in the church was at five or six years old. It ended when I was about 13: I just avoided going anywhere near these places where I knew these people would be or where I would bump into them.

At the time I was [*there is a long pause*]…I was dumbfounded, I just, you know, I couldn't understand why my father would not do anything about it, so I kept my mouth shut and with the constant grooming, it was something that I grew to…I even looked forward to it. They'd give me money or buy me things. I'd go home and I'd have, like, five shillings or whatever, and I'd hide half a crown and then, you know, I'd say that I'd found half a crown walking down the road.

I kind of learnt [in therapy in Grendon] that one of the things that I'd found with being abused as a child was that it was a substitute for care and affection. So, although these guys were abusing me they weren't hitting me, and I actually began to enjoy the abuse. I was being beaten at home and, basically, getting comfort from strangers. The thing with my own offending was I became aware that there was something going on in the background with my wife, that she was having an affair, and, it's not her fault, you know, but I think that triggered off me running back to somewhere where I felt comfortable and safe, but I'd switched roles: I was then the abuser.

I've had sex with older women and girls my own age. I didn't target children: the offending that I did was within my own family. I didn't look outside the family. I started off by touching my oldest daughter's genitalia and I think what it...the thing was that there was no [*he pauses a long while*]...she had no concept of anything about relationships or infidelities and things like that so, I guess, I saw her as being innocent. She was five then and this continued over years, and eventually it led up to me raping her. The offending was very persistent, it wasn't kind of here and there; it was, you know, I would say four or five times a week. The other daughter I'd had no sexual attraction for at all. It stopped when she was, I think, 17. She just said, 'No, I'm not doing this any more.'

I kind of think, wow, you know, where did that come from? I did read up a lot on sexual orientation offending, and things like that. One of the things that happens if somebody's abused at an early age – and I was in a position as well where I was having sex with girls my own age – but obviously too young to really understand what was going on – and, again, this is only something that I think about now, years later – there was a mirror in the room. I think there was a guy behind the mirror, taking photos. I think that kind of [*he pauses and sighs*] exposure to sexual behaviour at that early age will programme you to have a sexual attraction for a child. I'm not saying everybody that is abused goes on to become an offender – somebody who offends makes that choice, it's not something that they have no control over – but I think it is a definite link with child abuse. There were many times where I thought, 'I shouldn't be doing this, why am I doing this?' But, when the opportunity presented itself again the self-gratification was stronger than the 'Why am I doing this?' state of mind.

[*Why do you think you weren't willing to deal with your wife's affairs by having affairs yourself?*] It's a fair question and there is no real simple answer. I just think I was preoccupied with sex. It wasn't about the person, it was about me having an orgasm and I think that that was the thing. It was all about me and self-gratification, so it didn't matter whether it was my daughter or one of my wife's friends, the thing was I was having an orgasm.

I didn't have an attraction for children, not even when I was abusing my daughter, when she was five, six, seven, no, not apart from my daughter; not children, but teenage girls definitely, you know, older schoolgirls. I'd kind of look at them and think, 'Yeah.' No, I was doing what I wanted to do: there was no need for me to look elsewhere; I don't think that I needed that.

[*But having sex with one person, like your daughter, didn't rule out sex, or at least the sexual attraction to another, did it?*] Oh no, absolutely not. This is something obviously we talked a lot about in Grendon and I think there would have been a possibility that it would be risky, you would be more likely to get caught, so, I think I never investigated or thought about it really, because where I was, was safe.

I have never been attracted to children since the abuse stopped. If I go somewhere and I see parents with children, I move out the way. I think I can't be doing something. And again there is that other thing as well, you know like SIDs [Seemingly Irrelevant Decisions, an acronym in treatment]. So, if I was to sort of say, 'I don't have an attraction for this child, I don't see a problem with me associating with people with children,' the question really is then to ask is, 'If I've got any relationship, would I then target that child?' I have to be honest, I can't say that, but I definitely wouldn't [enter into such a relationship] because I don't know how it would pan out. So the thing is you don't get involved with people that have children. This is my kind of criteria: if I meet a woman, she must be single, no young children. Unfortunately, a lot of the time women my age now are grandparents, so to actually meet somebody where there's no connection with children is almost impossible. But, at the moment I'm not desperately lonely or need to be in a relationship. I have women friends; I don't have sex with them, but there are women that I speak to that are, you know, just people I speak to, and it's enough.

With my daughter the disclosure didn't happen until years later (I was about 46 or 47). Now when Jane said stop, I started focusing my attention on my younger daughter, and started trying to abuse her because she was a lot older by now, but she was, sort of, this is not going to happen. I touched her breasts a couple of times and she said. 'If you do that again I'm going to tell mum,' so that stopped. It was when my youngest daughter got married, about a year after, and she got pregnant, and had a little girl, and, I think, the fear was that I might abuse her child, and that was when the disclosure was made.

I pulled my wife up on her affair, but I didn't walk out because, well, there was nowhere else to go, whatever. We were still sleeping together, and, I guess, from my perspective, she was somebody I could have sex with. I hadn't been in love with her [when we met], and when she got pregnant, the only option then was to marry, so we got married. It wasn't a marriage of love or anything like that. But I grew to love her over the years as a person, but I was never really what you would call 'in love'.

She asked me to leave after the disclosure, and when I walked out of the front door I had absolutely no emotion about it at all. That was quite strange. I remember thinking at the time that I should be feeling something, but I'm not, you know, and, again, only kind of going through therapy and talking about this, I kind of realised that I didn't attach to people very well. Everything was always about me, it was always about what I wanted, how I wanted to feel, what I wanted to do: a total lack of empathy. I guess, too, with the way I was brought up, it isolated me from the rest of the world in a sense because I didn't learn proper social skills or learn to care and love was sex, violence was OK.

I wasn't attaching to people properly. I used to think empathy was feeling sad about things, you know, and maybe feeling sorry for myself – again, all about me. Empathy to me was a word but I didn't really understand it. I think it was probably after I'd been at Grendon for about two and half years, the light suddenly came on, and I just felt inside that I couldn't cope. For the first time in my life I actually saw what I'd done, and realised the impact of it. One of the justifications I used while I was abusing my daughter was, 'I'm OK, so she'll be OK,' and how distorted is that?

After the disclosure, I'd got to the point where I thought what's the point, kind of thing. I took a massive overdose and woke up in hospital. I'd had my stomach pumped I was sectioned [compulsorily detained in a psychiatric hospital] for 14 days for observation because when I woke up I'd really started having a go at 'em. You know, said I didn't do this for fun, this isn't, you know…like it's up to me what I do; if I wanna kill myself, I kill myself, and I don't want you touching me, you leave me alone. So obviously they sectioned me because they considered me a danger to myself. Retrospectively, that was me, in a sense, taking control. Had I succeeded, that would have really probably been extremely damaging to my daughters, and, after going through years of therapy, I'm glad that I didn't succeed. It's quite possible that they may have suffered from guilt, and feeling that my actions were their fault, which they weren't. It may well have left them feeling guilty that I'd killed myself over their disclosure. It wasn't a good thing to do.

[*But didn't the trial alert you to this at all? What was your insight then?*] It was almost like a numb process, it was something that was going on around me. I wasn't allowed to talk at all, I wasn't allowed to speak in court, and everything was done via solicitors and barristers. I pleaded guilty but some of the charges…the police kind of attached to what had happened. There was a point where my both my daughters' statements became identical and you would have had to be a fool not to have seen that this is just kind of pegged on the end, so I pleaded not guilty to things that I was not guilty of and pleaded guilty to everything that I'd done.

I did say to my solicitor that if they say that they're gonna contest this and they want my daughters in court, then I will plead guilty to those charges but I'm not guilty of them. She said, 'You can't do that, 'cause you've told me that you're not guilty,' and so there's this big hoo-hah about that and I said, 'My daughters are not going to stand up in a court, they've been through enough.' I didn't want any more crap for my daughters, I just thought, 'No, this is about me, this is something that I've done and I'm gonna go to prison for it.' I knew I'd go to prison, I kind of thought I'd probably get a 15-year sentence; as it was I got ten years, and I thought that was lenient, to be honest.

I did the SOTP, which was an interesting thing to go through, but I certainly don't think the SOTP on its own will change somebody's behaviour. It's a very good introduction into the idea of therapy. When I first went to Belmarsh, I was speaking to a male nurse. He'd asked me about how I'd ended up in prison and he was the person that told me about Grendon. He said that if I went to Grendon it would do me a lot of good; he thought I could engage there. He said, 'It's not an easy place, it's a tough prison, but, at the end of it, it can change your life.'

I heard that a lot of decisions were made by inmates [in Grendon]. It was a very democratic and a good system by actually allowing inmates to take responsibility for what they do. I moved to Grendon about two months after the SOTP, and went through a three-month induction. The whole thing was that there were no secrets, you know, you had to be open about your past. There were a lot of people there that were too scared to actually say that they were sex offenders. At the first meeting we had we were all asked to disclose why we were there, so you had armed robbers, drug dealers, people that were psychopathic, violent men. But the idea was that you would have to accept each other for who you were, as a person, not your offence. I had a hard time on the induction wing because I was honest about what I'd done. A few of the supposedly hard men – your armed robbers and whatever who think they're a cut above the rest – started targeting me, which I'd bring up at the wing meeting: 'Why are you pouring water under my door at night?' and that kind of thing.

I got a couple of smacks in the mouth, got a smack around the head with a boot. I was even attacked in [another prison] under the instructions of one of the wing officers. He told an inmate to put an electric iron that was hot on my face, and he was gonna do it but somebody else came onto the wing that just didn't put up with that kind of thing, and so that never happened, but it was very, very close.

One of the things about group therapy is that you're challenged by your peers and, within a prison system, child sex offenders are the lowest of the low, and even somebody who's raped an adult would consider themselves to be…well, I'm not a kiddie fiddler and things like that. So there were a lot of distortions. I was the only person on my group that would speak openly about my offending, but there were certain members that would attack me in the group, because it stopped people looking at them. Once I'd been there for a while and actually began to understand how distorted a lot of our thinking was, I was able to sort of say, 'No, what you're saying is not about me, it's about you,' and actually challenge some of the questions that were being put to me. There was a wing psychologist called Vicky and I can't thank her enough for some of the things that she pointed out to me. One day she said to me that I was too wrapped up in poor me. She said, 'How would it make you feel if you knew your daughter was standing there crying, next to you now, because you're not actually dealing with her, you're dealing with you? You're not even thinking about her.' That was the first time I'd been able to mentally visualise…kind of, you know…it's kind of when the light came on and I just thought, 'Does she do that? Does she do that every night?' And it was really a very, very hard thing to do.

I was debating about stringing myself up from the cell window because I didn't think I had the right to live; I didn't think what I'd done was something that just a prison sentence could deal with. I'd always maintain, even on the group, that people like me should be given the death penalty, and that's how I felt for a very long time, but again, that kind of thinking was challenged: isn't that the coward's way out? You're not man enough to actually do your sentence, and things like that. So I then made a kind of commitment I would carry on in therapy, but I would commit suicide after leaving prison.

A couple of times in Grendon I'd actually challenge myself. For example, I smoke, and while I was at Grendon I thought to myself, 'Well, if they're telling me I can change anything about me, I'm gonna stop smoking. If I cannot stop smoking, I'm not capable of changing, therefore I will have to leave Grendon.' I was a bit of an all-or-nothing kind of personality. I stopped smoking quite easily. It was significant to the point where I could say, 'Yeah, OK, I can do that, and if I can do that, then, obviously I'm capable of change,' so I continued. If you engage in therapy it's the hardest thing you'll do because most nights you're in absolute pieces. The therapy wasn't just on the group, it was all day all night. It was people talking to you: if you said something and you'd immediately be pulled up – 'What you mean by that?' If you walk into somebody's cell and they're watching a children's programme, then why are they watching that? So everything was challenged all the time. I guess it made me a lot stronger. One thing I have no problem with at all now is saying to somebody, 'I think what you're doing is wrong,' or challenging somebody, whereas before I'd always let things ride; anything for a quiet life.

One of the things I found was that were other child sex offenders, but their families continued to support them, so I actually felt quite isolated. No one in my family wanted anything to do with me. I mean, I wouldn't expect to be in touch with my children, they were my victims. I spoke to the wing chaplain and said that I was at a loss here, everybody seemed to have somebody (I think there were three of us on the wing that had absolutely no outside contact). It was suggested then that I get a prison visitor, so I had a woman, Marianne, who visited me. I was a bit suspicious because I thought, 'Why would you want to visit somebody like me?' She's extremely religious – not a thing that I'm into; I mean, going through the Catholic Church as I did, I'm an atheist and very, very happy about it – but Marianne was determined I needed saving. She was there for me all the time, and, funnily enough, after prison 'cause I'm still in touch with her. She has a bed and breakfast place, where I've gone and stayed when I've been visiting Grendon for open days when I go back to talk to the guys about how I'm finding life outside 'cause a lot of them are fearful of leaving prison. It was nice for me because I used to think like that [*laughs*] and it's nice for me to be able to go back and say, 'No, the exact opposite, there's support as long as you're keeping within your boundaries.' Now I've had a lot of support off the probation service and their interest is in helping me to lead a normal life.

I could speak to Marianne because one of the things that I'd said to her was that she comes to visit and then she's de-briefed about anything I say, but, she says, no, and anything I say to her that I don't want her to repeat she won't repeat it. I actually looked forward to her visits and the day I left prison she drove me to the hostel. She was on the phone quite a lot, making sure I was OK. People like that gave me a kind of hope – not everybody is a vigilante, not everybody has that kind of anger.

I think what happened was that I'd begun to realise it wouldn't matter if I did commit suicide – at the end of day my daughters would be the same. Also, one of things that I came to realise was that it would have been me sort of saying to them, 'Now look at what you've made me go and do'; it would be putting the blame on them. Once I'd got that, I just thought, 'I don't have that option any more, I can't commit suicide because I don't really have the right to do that, and that was a big turnaround.'

[*Was there any point at which you came from being this person who lacked empathy, who was numb about what happened, who was still very self-indulgent and self-interested, and started to develop empathy for others, and who, then, eventually (and I assume this is the case) found some way to like himself?*] A lot of it came from my Circle. When I got out of prison I had a lot of empathy for other people, but, unfortunately, none for myself. I could not cope with the outside world: I felt suddenly very isolated from being on a wing with 40 other guys, who all knew me, all knew what I'd done, but would still associate with me, and then to being out in a big, wide world that if anybody knew what I'd done, I would be in great danger. 'I'm gonna be on my own for the rest of my life, I'm not gonna have any friends, my whole life is about me being a sex offender.' But my Circle kind of began to turn that around and sort of say, 'Look, you've done a bad thing, but that's not all who you are.' It was just the fact that somebody would pick the phone up and say they wanted to go to the cinema and did I want to go along?

So to start off with it's kind of learning to know somebody because the initial thing is you see a bunch of people that know you're a sex offender. I was sitting there and thinking, 'Why are they doing this? Why on earth would they want to be involved with me?' I was honest about it, I felt pretty suspicious. 'I don't really get this,' I said. 'I understand the idea of a Circle, but why on earth would you want to associate with me?' Again, it was, 'The fact you're a person, you're a human being, you know, you're not your offences, you've done bad things, but that doesn't mean that you're all bad, and the good stuff is good.'

It took me a while to accept that, but, as I say, now I have various friends that I associate with. I wouldn't say I have any real close friends outside the Circle, but my Circle members actually know me, they know everything about me, and I feel safe with them. I can go to my Circle if I'm feeling down or, for argument's sake, I get invited to go somewhere, and I think, crap, there are going to be kids there – not that I think that I'm going to offend, but would it be an appropriate thing for me to go;

say somebody sees me there and misconstrues why I'm there – that's the kind of thing I can discuss.

I'm not craving sex. Funnily enough, for years my life was very, very sexually orientated, everything was about sex, I think my entire life was around sex, and now I find it's really low down on my priorities.

But you were asking me about Circles. Well, at Grendon we had the Quakers come on to the wing and they were actually doing a Circle project in the Thames Valley. They did a presentation about Circles and what they offered and how that would allow people that had left prison to learn to socialise and reintegrate into society safely. I spoke to them about it because I had no family or any support from outside other than Marianne. I thought this is probably something that I can make use of and would probably be very good for me. The other thing as well is that anything you wanna do, you have to talk to your group about it and the wing had to ask my group whether they would support the idea of me applying for a Circle, which they thought was a good idea. The wing backed me on that so I could apply. I was actually looking forward to being able to get out, meet these people and start putting some sort of a life back together.

From the Circle's perspective it is about behaviour management, you know, to watch out for any warning signs. I'd been in prison a long time, and you become institutionalised, and it happens very quickly. I remember when I went into prison it was extremely traumatic. I had no experience of it, it was a totally alien environment and most of the guys in there had been in and out all their lives so they kind of knew the ropes, and took advantage of anybody that didn't. But coming out of prison is actually as traumatic as going in. I got on a bus and it was £2 for a bus ride, and I think when I went to prison it was 30p! It's just little culture things like that. I couldn't get any money out the bank because the bank recognised me as having been in prison and when I came out of prison they wanted passport, driving licence, things like that, to prove that I was me. That was a nightmare to get back into the system, but my Circle helped with that.

But it was a difficult kind of thing because the Circle would occasionally kind of come up with 'What're you fantasising about?' or 'Do you go down to the park? Do you look at children?' That's part of their remit, that's about the protection side of the Circle because it is a Circle of accountability *and* support. The accountable part is they want to make sure that your behaviour isn't suspicious and if it was, they would flag it up with the police, or probation, and the likelihood is that

I would end up being back in prison. I've always seen my Circle actually more of the support side, because I've had no fears about reoffending.

The day I moved into my flat from the hostel, and I shut the front door, I thought, 'I'm on my own,' and it was the ultimate cut-off: you're out of prison. If I didn't have the Circle I think depression would have spiralled downwards, eventually to the point when I would've gone, 'What's the point?' I have suffered with depression a lot, most of my life, and, again, I think that's related to the way I was brought up, or beaten up, or dragged up. I suffered a lot of guilt over the offending and still do. In an ideal world, it would be taken away, but you can't turn the clock back, so I'd I have a tremendous amount of guilt about my offending, and, yeah, it's something on my mind a lot.

One of the things about Circles is that, like, birthdays, I'll flag it up to them and say, 'Oh, it's one of my daughters' birthdays coming up next week.' You can't help thinking and hoping she's OK, and not being part of their lives can be very difficult. With Circles there's somebody I can talk to, somebody I can spend the time with. It's about asking if I fancy going places, giving me things to do, things that'll occupy myself, so I can actually enjoy getting out and about. Basically, I can go anywhere I please but if I'm on my own all the time then it doesn't…one of the things I've learnt is you can be in the most beautiful place on the planet, but if what's going on up here [*points to his head*] is in pieces, then it's gonna be in pieces no matter where you are. So it's a case of sort of saying I need a bit of support in just being able to engage in things that most people take for granted, like going out for a coffee or for a meal or seeing a film, going round a flea market. They're ordinary things but extremely precious, because that's somebody that's not giving up their time because they have to, they're giving up their time because they want to. That's incredible for them to actually sort of say, 'I wanna spend time with you.'

I don't think Circles would suit everybody. Seven out of ten sex offenders would work OK in Circles, the rest would play the part, but actually, you know, carry on offending. Sex offenders are very good at covering their tracks. (I was offending against my daughter for years and nobody suspected that that was going on.) The whole thing is about secrecy and manipulation, and sex offenders – strangely enough and people might find it odd to hear – come across as extremely nice people, friendly, intelligent, and the sad thing it can be anybody. In my case it's a father; it could be an uncle, a mother, an aunt, an uncle, could be the guy that lives next door, who just seems to enjoy your children.

The trouble is there is absolutely no way that anybody can point a finger and say, 'That guy is a paedophile.' It's just that you wouldn't recognise it. They don't go around with leering kind of looks on their faces: they're people like you and me.

Grendon worked for me and it's worked for lots of others. I go back for the social evenings and open days because Grendon changed my life. I owe them a debt of gratitude. Had I just gone through the prison system and got spat out the other end, I think the likelihood is that I would've engaged in the criminal lifestyle, not necessarily sexual offending but I would have felt an outcast and, what's the point, I might as well just go for what I can get, you know. Grendon gave me the opportunity to actually step back and say, 'I have choices in my life, I'm not ruled by a sex drive, I'm not ruled by all about me, and I can actually sit down and think, "I wanna go and do this: is it risky?"' I wanna play it safe so, with me, it's always caution. I'm very, very aware of what made me perceived as a risk and I might not think it's a risk, but I then question myself.

With Circles, I can talk if I'm feeling down, or I feel suicidal, or, actually, 'I feel really great today,' or 'You know, I've done this, I'm really happy.' They're on the ball with what's going on in my life. I get texts backwards and forwards from [names Circles volunteers] and I just think well, you know, these people spend time for me. [A volunteer's] job is extremely time-filling, but if I need her she's always there. [Another volunteer] is the same, and at the moment [he] is going through this operation, the second one – he's had cancer, he needs support – and it's a bit of a role reversal but I go up to the hospital, and if there's anything that I can do, then I do it. He was out of hospital last year after he had his bladder removed and he was not in a good way, and I was showering him, I was washing him, sorted his clothes out for him, making sure he'd got something to eat; so care goes both ways. They become friends, and OK, you know, even though they're friends, if I was doing anything that they thought was risky, they'd still pick up the phone because that's what a friend would do. A friend would say you're actually not firing on all cylinders and I think you need some help, and help might be picking up the phone and calling the police. Circles are there for the public and they're there for the core member. I've got a brilliant Circle.

Life as it's going on at the moment is OK. I would love to be in a loving relationship with a woman that I could fall in love with and have a proper relationship with for the first time in my life. I guess that's probably the only thing that I'm missing. I've got great friends, I've got a lot of support, I've gotta lot of care.

Prison was probably the best thing that ever happened to me. I know it probably sounds strange considering how nasty prison can be, but it gave me the opportunity to say, 'This is me, this is my life, this is how I grew up, this is what I became, and this is me now.' I always consider myself an ex-offender, because I've no desire to offend again, or, you know, create any victim in any way, sense, form or shape. I don't verbally abuse people, I don't do things that might upset or hurt somebody. I kind of work on the premise that I think about what I do, I think about what I say, and if I can't do something good for somebody, I won't do 'em any harm. That's kind of how I am now and I know that I'll never go back to prison, I know that I'll never reoffend again. But because of my past, nobody can ever believe me 100 per cent, they always have to have that element of doubt, and I accept that because that's the sensible thing to do. I think every sex offender that sits in front of a parole board, a probation officer or a police PPU [Public Protection Unit] team will say, 'I'm never gonna reoffend,' and I think that's something they must hear all the time, and so they can't believe when people say that, 'cause they can't take the chance that that person's just singing from the hymn book. I don't particularly care whether anybody thinks I might reoffend again or not: as far as I'm concerned that's their issue to deal with. But, for me, I know who I am: probably for the first time in my life I'm comfortable with me. That's me come a long way. I hated me, I resented me. If I'd been physically able to, I could have beaten myself to a pulp, but, you know, I'm, yeah, I'm pretty OK now.

David Dawson: 'It's like lighting candles in a very dark room'

David Dawson meets me at a rural railway station in a small town in the west of England. He is wearing dark glasses because, he explains, he is known by a taxi driver and the man who runs the burger van, both parked nearby. Both know of his offence, but do not know that he lives in the town. Yet he refers to others in the town, whom he knows from his time as a dustman and who also know of his offence, and also to the many members of his local Anglican church, with whom he has been open about what he did. He refers to them as friends and tells how a group of the latter meet in his small flat on a pleasant new development. (His wife and two stepdaughters, against one of whom he offended, still attend a house church in a town nearby; they all used to attend as a family.)

David is 44, has been married three times (he is just about to go through his latest divorce) and has five children: one with a girlfriend when he was 21 (his daughter is now 24), and two each with his first and second wives. He also has two grandchildren, but has only seen one of them and then only twice. He has no contact with any of his wives or his children. Photographs of all his children line the walls of his sitting room.

Both his parents are alive but he has had no contact with them for nearly two years – they do not reply to his phone messages or emails – or with his two younger sisters. He says that they have never been close. When he was 11 he tried to have sex with them.

He was born in the north-west, and his father, a musician, drank heavily and had a gambling habit. He beat him severely, instigated and egged on by his mother. His social services records indicate he was abused before he was 12 but he has no recollection of this. There may have been some sexual activity with his father when he was 11 and with his mother when he was in his teens. There was also sexual activity with two female care workers when, aged 14, he was in a children's home. He was anally raped by another boy, also in a children's home. It was reported, but nothing was done, he says. After that he began to self-harm and has also attempted suicide on several occasions (the last time in 2009). He was expelled from school, ran away from home and spent three years in local authority care. He was sentenced to six weeks' 'short, sharp shock' in a detention centre when he was 16 for theft and later served 15 months of a three-year sentence for assault with intent to rob. At 15 he was glue sniffing and later he took other drugs including cannabis, LSD and heroin. He has engaged in much petty crime. He has had one or two gay sexual experiences (including in a probation hostel) but puts this down to heavy drinking. He has held various unskilled jobs. This has been a life, he has written in a long, uncompleted manuscript autobiography, 'of sexual confusion and perversion'. At 18 he came forward at a rally held by the evangelist Billy Graham and he appears to have retained his faith. He twice sought help for his sexual behaviour from GPs before he committed his offences, but never received any. In 2005 he was arrested on 13 charges, going back two or three years, of inappropriate sexual behaviour with the younger of his two stepdaughters. He denied the charges, which were dropped. He underwent 90 hours of therapy and returned to the family in December 2006. He now admits that 'some' of the allegations were true and he later admitted to one of them and was convicted of this offence when, in 2009, he received a non-custodial sentence for a separate batch of offences regarding the same stepdaughter (the children were then 12 and 14). He received a three-year community order. David has now stopped drinking, smoking and taking drugs and leads a celibate life. He works as a cleaner, having told his employer about his offence. David's distortions and his tendency to rationalise and justify his behaviour would be addressed at the sex offender treatment programme he was to begin soon after the time of the interview (October 2010). When we met he had been a Circle core member for five to six months.

It was in 2003 when it started. My sexual relationship with my wife had diminished so I started masturbating more, fantasising and having images of my stepdaughters being naked. I'd start fantasising about touching them and that's when the problem really started.

I knew it was wrong and it felt very uncomfortable and I did look on the Internet to try and get help, but I couldn't get any. I was too ashamed to talk to anybody about it and that's why I went to the doctor's. I told my wife as well; I said that I was having fantasies over her daughters. I was very honest with her. The doctor was quite shocked and when I asked him if there anything he could give me to control my sexual urges, he said the only thing that he could do was to refer me to a psychologist, which never came about unfortunately.

I tried controlling the thoughts, the fantasies in my mind, by trying to fantasise about my wife and other adults, other than my stepdaughters. I'd get up in the morning and I'd go out to work (used to drive a lorry) and all day long I'd be repenting it and say, 'I don't want to do this any more, that's the end of it now, I've done it, that's it, I'm gonna stop, no more.' I'd go back to the house. But, as soon as I got into bed, all the desires would come back. It's not as if I got up in the morning and planned to abuse in the evening. It's not as though every day, you know, I'd be thinking, 'Yeah, this is what I wanna do.' It wasn't like that, it was more a battle of 'I don't wanna do this, I don't want these desires or these thoughts or these fantasies, I want it all to go away, I don't want it.' I did have a conscience, a massive conscience. If I hadn't had a conscience, I think, I'm pretty sure, I would have abused a lot more than what I did.

I think I've got an addictive nature and everything was for my own gratification. Yeah, I would definitely say that the feelings and emotions

I had were that I was more important than anything else and the same with my relationships as well: it was really important for me to be treated as the most important thing since sliced bread, not an egoistic thing, but I just needed that comfort and that safety and to be looked after.

No, never; I never felt attracted to other children. Never, and still not now. It was only within the family and only my two stepdaughters. We used to have my own children stay as well and I never had any desires towards them. My stepdaughters' friends used to come and stay, and never any desires towards them either.

Before it happened, things were OK with my wives. It was fine, and I got on really well with them. My first wife and my second wife are really good friends now, but we all used to get on really well together and then, obviously, when my offences came to light they didn't want to know me, and kept me away from the children. When I was separated from my first two wives, I would still see all the children every two or three weeks and they used to stay for weekends.

Oh, I knew it was wrong, yeah.

[So why did you persist?] I don't really know the psychology behind it at all. If I knew that I guess I could undo whatever was done, but I really don't know. I knew it was wrong obviously. It's a very selfish kind of…you know, 'My needs are greater than anybody else's.' When I first went back home in 2006 after all the therapy, for the first six months everything was great between me and my wife, and my stepdaughters called me dad, my, our sex life was good, but then after a while she [his wife] started withdrawing that, so what I did then was I'd ask her to masturbate me. I didn't want to do it myself because I was frightened of the fantasies coming back, but she wouldn't, so I was left to my own means. That's when the fantasies started again over my stepdaughters, and all day long I'd be, 'I'm not gonna do it, I don't wanna do it,' because thousands of times I could have offended and I didn't. I really didn't want to, and I tried really hard not to but, sometimes, when at night time I'd be in bed, my stepdaughter'd come in to watch telly with me, I couldn't resist if there was an excitement inside me that I just couldn't make go away.

My stepdaughter used to pretend she was asleep, when I used to offend – it was about four times [on the occasion of the second offences], I think. No, I never said nothing at all [about her not telling], I didn't have to, 'cause I just knew that she wouldn't say anything.

Of course, I fantasised over them both. I probably could have groomed the older one for intercourse, but I knew she'd say something, but my younger stepdaughter, there was something about her that I just knew that she wouldn't say anything, so I didn't have to threaten her, I didn't have to say, you know, 'I'll go prison,' or 'Me and your mum will split.' I didn't have to say anything at all. It was just very subtle grooming over a period of time.

How it came to light was that my younger stepdaughter gave a note to her older sister to say that 'Dad has been making me do things to him and has been touching me.' I knew then that they knew, and they went and told their mum. Their mum said she wanted me out of the house by the time she got back. So I was faced with three choices. I bought a length of rope and a bottle of whisky because I thought I'd just hang myself – there's no point going on. Or I thought I could do a runner and try and get away, or I'd go and hand myself into the police, make a full confession and try and get help, and that's what I did. The police were quite surprised because they'd never had someone come in before and make a confession before a complaint had been made, so I think that kind of helped me in my court case really, 'cause I knew that I had a problem and needed help with it.

[*You say you had no sexual desire for children except for your two stepdaughters, so let me put it this way: if you wanted sexual satisfaction why didn't you have an affair or go to a prostitute?*] The psychology behind it, that's probably quite odd to be honest. In the past when things haven't worked out, with a partner, I've just gone somewhere else, and my ex-wives and ex-girlfriends, they can all give testimony to that. I've never left one and been on my own, I've always gone from one to the other, but with my third wife I didn't wanna do that any more, I was tired of starting again, and I really wanted to make it work, so I wouldn't have an affair, I wouldn't leave, and I kept thinking I wanna try and make this work. Unfortunately because I didn't have an affair and there was still a need to be met, I focused towards my stepdaughters.

[To have gone with a prostitute] felt like more of a betrayal. I know that sounds really odd, because I know that, I mean now, why didn't I? I wish I had done, or anything, anything other than my stepdaughters, and I don't know why I didn't and the only thing I can think of is that it felt like more of a betrayal if I'd have had an affair. I don't understand it at all, but it just felt like…see, with my other wives, OK, I would never dream…I mean, we had nephews and nieces and that, and I'd never dream of abusing. I would just move on to another woman, but with my third wife I didn't wanna do that, I was tired of starting again, tired of divorces and remarriage and relationships. I wanted to make it work so I was determined to stay within the family environment, whatever it took. I just think that once sex was taken away from me – I mean that was an important part of my life – I didn't wanna go elsewhere, I didn't wanna have an affair, I didn't wanna go with a prostitute, and it just became, one of the stepdaughters, I just became very close to her, she became very close to me. It was a very thin line, and I just…I crossed over the line.

Do I feel as though I'm different because I have only sexually desired those two children? I'm definitely a child sex offender, I mean obviously the rest of my life I will be, as I am a drug addict, as I am an alcoholic, as I am a smoker (I've just stopped), but I don't believe I'm a predatory sex offender. I know I'm not because I don't look at children and fantasise over them, I've got no desires to do anything to them, so I think I'm the same as I'm a child sex offender, yes; as to whether I'm predatory, no, I think I'm different.

I've been what you might call empathetic to people at a distance like on television or something you read in the newspaper, but when it's close I'm not; I can't feel it. It was like that with my stepdaughter. I used to look at her and wonder what she was feeling and thinking, but it was more a curiosity. I know she must have been feeling confused and probably feeling dirty about what had happened and it still wasn't enough to stop me. There was no sorrow that was so extreme that it made me wanna stop, even though I knew it was wrong. I would like to meet my stepdaughters and I'd like them to get angry at me and tell how they felt and I think that would help me empathise.

With all my confused sexual history as a youngster, I never really saw myself as a victim, anyway. It was just something that happened in my life. I never thought it gave me any problems or anything, it was just a part of my life and that was it. It was only through my probation officer that I came to realise that it did have an effect on my upbringing and on my life. That's not blaming anybody because I am to blame, and that's not detracting, you know, from my offences: I know I did wrong, I've got free will, but it did have an influence on my childhood and on my adult life, but I never realised that so I couldn't relate that to my offending. That has helped me a lot.

It was my dad who was really brutal but my mum would wind me up, she would do things and I'd get really wound up and I'd react to it, and I would get sent to bed. Then when my dad would come in, she'd say, 'Oh, he's been playing up', et cetera, and my dad would come up and he'd take it out on me.

It never happened with my sisters, no, they were always the salt of the earth, but I never wanted to come across as being 'I'm the victim', so I never felt that I had the right to blame anything. It was always my fault, it was always me. Sometimes my sisters did wrong but I still got punished for it, because I was the oldest child. There's a part of me that hates my parents, I am so angry and hate them so much. I never feel like that about people. I can be very loving and forgiving, kind and generous, but towards my parents, I hate them. But still, when I was on talking terms with them, I'd still love 'em, I'd still go up and spend Christmas with them and holidays. So although I hated them, there's another part of me that was very loyal to them and loving. In my social services history it says that I still maintained a loyalty towards my parents and even to this day I still kind of feel that.

When I was in prison in 1987, I remember – I'd not long become a Christian – praying and asking why have I had the life that I've had. Why? And then I started kind of regressing over it and that's when memories were starting to come back to me that had been oppressed [sic] – you know, in reference to my dad, my parents. I think that was probably the only time where I asked the question why, and then I came up with the memories to do with my own childhood. But, then, after that when I got out of prison, I thought, 'Well, that's it now: I remembered it, it's dealt with, that's the end of it.' But, I mean, sitting here today I know it wasn't, I know that something – I don't know how it works but deep psychology, subconscious or something – it was all still ticking away there and affecting the decisions that I was making.

When I first went to see my probation officer, I said to him that the only way I could explain it is like this – that my mind works as a 43-year-old man, I can buy a car, I can drive a car, I can pay a mortgage, I can hold down a job, but emotionally I feel as though I haven't reached puberty. I felt like that for a long time, but I could never explain to anyone and when I told him that, he wasn't surprised because what happens is when you're younger and something traumatic happens in your life, he said, your emotions close down and it's like you still hold on to the childhood emotions until your adult life. That was like a blast of revelation, and no one had ever explained that to me before, so I could actually look back and say, 'Yeah, that's kind of where it did go wrong, I guess.' That was probably the biggest thing in my life, that was a turning point for me that helped me understand things. Now I feel emotionally as though I've passed puberty. I feel like, emotionally, I'm grown up and maturing, because of the help I've had through Circles and from my probation officer.

I had become a Christian three years earlier with Billy Graham at Anfield [football stadium, Liverpool] but it was in prison, really, that was when I thought wow, you know, this is right for me and so I started reading the Bible and going to church.

I know what I did should have been the last thing on my mind, but I'm still human at the end of the day. I only stopped taking drugs five years ago. I've been a Christian for 20-odd years, but because I'd become a Christian didn't mean that overnight I'm gonna be Mother Teresa, perfect. I still had problems that I believe now stem from my childhood, and it's just taken a long, long time to recognise and deal with them.

[*If tomorrow your wife said, 'Come back and live with us,' do you think those desires would be there again? I'm not asking whether you could control them, I'm asking if they'd be there.*] I think, yes, they would be, depending on the circumstances. Like before, when circumstances were right between the first batch of offending and the second batch, there was no desires. It all stopped because my need was being met. I think if I went back to my wife, and my stepdaughters were there – obviously they're a bit older now – in all honesty I believe, yes, I believe if things weren't right, as they weren't before, I believe the desire would come back. But I haven't had intercourse for close to two years and stopped masturbating August 2009, whereas before the sexual desire controlled me, that's how it felt anyway. Now I feel as though I control my sexual desires, which are very, very minimal – at the moment anyway – but I'm not as blind as to think, well that's it, there's a cure and it could happen again, I don't know, I hope not, but…

When I joined the church, I told them. Obviously I told the vicar originally. He, in turn, told the church warden who's [the church member responsible for safeguarding], and then there were a few people that I knew I could trust and to me were good role models, which is what I needed, so I told them. I think there's about 30 people now within the church environment that know my offence and that made me feel safer. Not only does it light more candles in my little, dark room, it also makes me feel safer as well because it means that people are watching me and monitoring me, so no one can then accuse me of anything that I haven't done. With a couple of them there has been [an informal Circle] and in fact we had a meal here recently and they actually are gonna volunteer to become Circle volunteers.

I've been for quite a few interviews and I've been open and honest and the interview goes well until you make a disclosure and then they don't wanna know, and very, very negative feelings develop: instantaneous switch against you.

My parents haven't spoken to me since what happened. I rang them up and told them, and the last I heard was from my wife right at the beginning of 2009 – I was living in a caravan and she said that she'd had a phone call off my mother, who had said that for 43 years she'd put up with me and was kind of pulling me to bits. I haven't heard anything from my sisters at all for probably two or three years. Oh, they'll know, yeah, and I'm pretty sure all my family know.

[*How did you know about Circles?*] I was seeing my probation officer and he said there's a charity called Circles. When I found that people were trained and provided [and that you could not choose your Circle], I found that really off-putting at first because they weren't people that I knew or trusted. I didn't know anything about them, who they were, and then to find they were going to take minutes of meetings and things like that, which I kind of had a problem with at the start. But I could see the value of it. It was like this: when I went to live in the caravan [after leaving the family home], that was the end of it for me. What was the point of living? There's no point, for the rest of my life. But, again, I thought I was going to prison and for the rest of my life I'm going to be branded as a sex offender; there was no light at the end of the tunnel. Then certain people from my old church came alongside me and just loved me and helped me and gave me reassurance that I can still have a life even with this label; it was like lights going on in a dark room, bit by bit. So I could see the value of Circles, how it helps somebody that's got no hope.

It's like living in a very, very dark room. The lowest of the low, you can't get no lower than sexual offending, and society obviously makes that even worse by their attitude towards it, but when one person, just one person, no matter who they are, shows some form of kindness, a smile, and knowing about the offences but not condoning them – when someone says what you've done is wrong, but still we're gonna come alongside you and help you rehabilitate, teach you control, and try and give you a life back, that's like a candle being lit, some big candles, some little candles, but it's a candle being lit. And every time somebody knows, but doesn't turn their back, helps you along the way, that's another candle that's been lit and eventually it's like a dark room that's starting to be lit and you can see the way out, and that's what it feels like, and Circles, as with my church friends, Circles is very, very much like that. It's lighting candles in a dark room and it reduces the chances of reoffending, I believe.

The first thing I did was I asked them. I said, 'Why do you want to do this?' And the response was that they just believed that people can change. I just thought, wow, that's...you know...just...the majority of the world wanna lynch you, and for someone to come alongside, it's like ...it's really giving you hope.

I knew that the end goal would be obviously to reduce and maybe, hopefully, one day eliminate offending, but also to help me as well, along the way. But even now it still shocks me: I still can't understand why somebody would want to do that, but I know the value of it and I know the fruits of it.

I think of my circumstances as different [from many other such offenders] because I didn't come out from prison [without friends], I had friends already, but there is a value to having Circles even for me, because it helped me to look at women in a different light because all my Circle members are female. Now in the past, when I first started Circles, I complained a bit because I wanted a male volunteer, who hopefully would see it from a man's point of view, but it actually worked out better. With my Circle members, it was the first experience I had of being in female company and seeing them more as mature adults, human beings, exactly the same as, you know, me kind of thing, so I didn't see them in any kind of sexual light.

I don't think I ever had a mature relationship with a woman. I think my relationships in the past have been very immature and childish and that's why they've never worked, because rather than approach a thing with a mature emotional attitude, I break things, smash things, run away and run off to the next one. Now I see things a lot more differently, through probation, self-awareness, some form of self-healing, and through my Circle.

The therapy [after the first offences] did help because before I went back to the family home it gave me what they call tools in my toolbox and a prevention from reoffending plan as well, and that helped me a lot because if any problems were going to develop I could control them and put things in place to prevent anything going wrong. But then, after a while, the desire just got stronger and stronger so in the end I'm not even opening my toolbox.

I would say, even if you don't go to prison and even if you've got a community and a circle of friends, even family support as well, Circles is very valuable. It offers accountability, an unbiased point of view and a voice as well. I know that there's some form of accountability with family and friends but you're close to them, so it could be more possible to manipulate them – not that I would. But with the Circle volunteers, it's a lot more difficult to do that because they're not friends, they're there to monitor, to advise and to help, but in a friendly way.

I'm worried about [starting the SOTP] only in a sense that I've never done group therapy, I've only ever done a kind of a one-to-one. I try really hard to avoid anything of a sexual nature and I don't like the thought of sitting in a room and listening to other people telling me about their offences, because I don't want anything going into my mind that might trigger anything. I welcome learning about empathy and myself, et cetera, and the psychology and human nature side of it, the opportunity for someone to give me means to help me reduce, stop, prevent, reoffending.

I like where I'm at, I'm in control of my mind, I don't have fantasies any more, I don't have raging sexual urges and desires. I have got plans, I'm hoping in the future to be self-employed – I do cleaning so I am thinking about starting a cleaning agency – so, I mean, that side of it will be OK, I hope. I've been on my own for a year and half now and I have female friends – that's the difference now – the female friends, I don't see 'em as a potential girlfriend, wife, partner, someone to have sex with, any more. I like them very, very much as friends. Relationship-wise, who knows? I'm still married and I still wear my wedding ring, but I doubt very much I'll ever get back with my wife. I'd like to, but I don't think that'll ever happen, but relationship-wise in the future, who knows, maybe one day.

I tried to get in touch with people, with ex-girlfriends, to apologise for my behaviour. I treated one really, really bad, and I wanted to apologise so I did. I traced her, found out where she was, got in touch, apologised, and since then we've been in touch for the last six months. I've been up there to stay, and she's been down here to stay and we've got a really, really good friendship that's developed. It's great, it's very mature. I've never had that before: it's always been sex on the first night and three months later I've married them and nine months later there's a baby, whereas now it's different. I ain't in no rush – two, three, four, five years, who knows?

Ian Morrison: 'I will not produce any more victims'

Ian Morrison's voice is soft and he speaks in slow, measured tones. He answers thoughtfully but tends not to expand unless asked to do so, though he never refuses to answer or seeks to evade a question. He is a large man, a stature that seems at odds with the pathos of the life he describes. His mother and father worked on the buses. Aged 50 and born in Scotland, Ian refers to his childhood as 'hell' – the 'beltings and slappings' administered by his father, in which his mother colluded, even if she did not participate. He is one of four children, only one of whom has not been estranged from their parents and each other. In 1992 he received two years' probation with condition of residence for indecent assault on a 15-year-old boy. In 2004 he received an eight-year prison sentence (of which he served five and a half years with release on licence) for gross indecency with five boys over a two-year period. He describes his apprehension as 'a relief'.

Ian had recently made contact with his parents and his younger brother. His parents do not know about his offending, and his younger brother has rejected him because of what he did, but has promised not to tell their parents. He had little to do with his elder brother and sister because, as children, the age gap was too great – one is six years older, the other eight years. His elder brother has not returned his telephone calls. When he was 12, his then brother-in-law came to stay and sexually abused him. He never told anyone, partly, he says, because he believes no one would have believed him. At about this time he realised that he was gay and while he resisted the abuse at first, he says he 'came to like it'. He was a lonely boy, with no friends of his own, but who made friends with the friends of his younger brother. He thinks now that he did so partly because he wanted to control them.

He left school at 15 and worked in a number of jobs, including as a taxi driver and a lorry driver. He joined the RAF until he was forced to leave for being disruptive after four years. Unable to come out about his sexuality, he says he married to conform and did so twice. The first marriage, which was unconsummated, lasted only weeks. He was with his second wife for a year, during which time their now 20-year-old daughter was conceived. He says that he also tried to conform – 'to blend in' – by becoming a scout leader and a youth leader, but he thinks he may also have done this to allow him contact with young boys. His only gay relationships have been brief sexual encounters. 'My whole life was a lie…I couldn't be myself.'

Until he left prison last year he had never had a mature (non-sexual) relationship with an adult: even his new neighbours he avoided at first. Now Ian says he is happy just being able to talk to another person in a normal way. Only 'one or two' people know about what he did and he has stayed friendly with them. He does not know where his wives or his daughter live but he is sure that his second wife has told his daughter about his offences. Nevertheless, he hopes that one day his daughter will want to contact him. He lives in a privately rented studio flat in the south-east of England.

My younger brother got a lot of the attention, and my elder brother and sister were out of the picture; they were grown up. I spent all my holidays that I could with my gran. She brought me up, in a sense, through the holidays; she didn't like the way I was treated. My dad belted us, slapping us, a lot of punishment. I was a horrible kid.

My mother backed him in what he did, but she never actually put a hand on me. It was always, 'I'll tell your father' whatever and he'd take his belt off. My little brother was sort of devious in that sense 'cause if anything went wrong it would be my fault so he'd take liberties.

At school, we were into drugs all the time. Since, like, primary school, I never had many friends, I used to rely on my brother's friends sometimes.

Kids are the cruellest things around, and being called a poof and everything else I actually thought they knew, in a sense. It drove me nuts. It made me...I was alienated against a lot of people, I mean the only real friend that I had that last year in the school was in the air cadets that I joined, and there weren't many [friends] but there were a couple, good friends but none of them knew I was gay. I couldn't tell them, but I had a lot of loneliness, a lot of loneliness. Nobody to speak to about how I felt; I didn't know what to do. And when I got abused by my brother-in-law [when Ian was 12] I realised I was gay. I couldn't tell anybody else. There were a couple of threats [by the brother-in-law] against my younger brother, but I actually got to like it in a sense. There was a bit of resistance initially but I got attention and so I kind of liked it.

But then, after, it was just the odd one-night stand if I found somebody who was gay and again they were all about my age anyway. I never had sex with an adult, if you like, apart from the abuse.

I went on a job creation scheme after school – I left in 1968 when I was 15 and a bit – and then joined the RAF but I got thrown out after four years, mainly for destructive behaviour, immaturity. I couldn't follow orders. What did I do then? Bummed around England really, just looking for work, and picked up little jobs, like a taxi driver, but then met my first wife. I met her on the CB [citizens' band radio] of all things. It was false because I was gay, but I couldn't admit I was gay so to fit in and blend in I married her. I didn't want to tell her about my childhood. My whole life was a lie. Any gay relationships I had were just a couple of sort of stands, I couldn't be myself. The marriage probably failed because I didn't give her any attention and I didn't want sex. The second [marriage], again we blended in because I settled a bit in the village and became a youth leader, scout leader and we started to fit in.

I allowed [the offences] in a sense because I believed that that's what [the boys] wanted, 'cause they were from a disturbed background, but their background wasn't gay and I explained it by the fact that they wanted to be with me, so I was happy with it. On the second occasion the boys were neighbours. I mean, I knew it was wrong, but I felt that the only relationship I could have was with young people who wouldn't judge me.

There were a number of times when I wanted to stop it and move on, but the urge to have sex was just too big and I gave myself permission each time. I did feel guilty afterwards, as there's always that fear you'll get caught or one of the boys' parents will find out. The only thing I used to discuss with the boys was that if I'm ever caught I'll go to prison, that sort of thing, to try to lay the guilt on them in a sense. [With the second offence] with one boy, I tried to stop him taking drugs. I discovered he was taking tablets and he'd done a runner, came back. He said [to the police], basically, it wouldn't have happened if I hadn't touched him. I believe that they said the other boy didn't actually want to press charges. Whether it was a loyalty thing or fear, I don't know, but there was a sense of relief for me.

I did speak to a doctor [about it] once during the last offence and he dismissed it: when I said, should I have an attraction for young boys, he said I was just depressed.

With the first offence I did the six-week [sex offender] course which didn't really delve into details like it did when I did the SOTP [sex offender treatment programme in prison] with the second offence. It delved more into your life, but the second one was very helpful.

Initially, there was a bit of shock at some offences [detailed by others on the course]. One or two of them were really young children, but I learnt not to judge. There were a couple of offences where they believed that they were not in the wrong, you know, the child was in the wrong, I wasn't keen on that but I wouldn't go into details because you're not allowed to challenge in a negative way. We obviously offered pointers just to say, 'Well, don't you actually think they were distressed?' or that type of thing, but you never actually pointed fingers; you're not allowed to. I wouldn't allow people to judge me, but they raised awareness of what you were doing, and what you've done, the damage you've done. I don't look at anybody's offence and think that they are worse or better than mine. At the end of the day it's against the law, you've got victims.

What was good [about the course] was it made you look at yourself. I never really thought about victims before, to be honest, as I always believed – I wanted to believe that, anyway – that that's what they wanted. But to see the damage done, the ripple effect with the families, friends, everybody. And I see about being able to look at myself, why I should be honest with myself, and it's helped tremendously so I was able to be myself. I don't have to lie to anybody, make up stories about my family or anything else. I can't judge people who put up a fence but before I was making up stories about my family, my life, everything.

It has changed my life. When I was lying and telling stories I had a few gay friends and a few straight friends (not that they can ever meet, you know, as it'd be disastrous), but now people accept me for who I am, and I don't have to make up stories. I'm gay, live with it. And as far as the offences go, obviously people don't know – well, there's one or two people who do – but what I mean is that I socialise with people that have been on the course. If I ever meet new people I won't come out and say, 'I'm gay,' but if it comes up in conversation that I'm gay, I've no fear, whereas before I had the fear of being beaten the hell out of. There's a lot of groups that hate it, but if they don't like it, then it's fine by me, as long they don't turn it to hate crime themselves, but I've never experienced that.

[*You still have a sexual attraction for younger people. How do you deal with that?*] I deal with that with a lot of self-talk [part of the process known as 'cognitive restructuring' which involves self-questioning, challenging one's thoughts and feelings], saying it's wrong, but it'll probably not ever go away. It's just now feeling comfortable really with kids, teenage boys anyway. I've worked with kids but that wasn't always a sexual thing. I did a lot of work with kids, but obviously that's out of the question now, but I walk through the streets sometimes and see somebody that looks attractive – I just dismiss that now. As I say, there's a lot of self-talk, change the subject, not avoidance as such but dealing with it, 'Why do you think like that?' and so on. It's an avoidance strategy [if he comes in contact with boys] – I go down town and you get kids come up to you and it's 'Sorry,' I've said, 'I've no time, sorry,' just carry on. There's no one of any age like that where I live, so that's a good thing.

Self-talk is important to me. I question everything I do. I used to be so impulsive; I'd just get on and do it. Now I actually step back, look at myself, look at the possible outcomes.

[*Do you find that it contradictory that, on one hand, you're harming children, but, on the other hand, you wanted to help them by working with them?*] That was one of the biggest puzzles of my life. There was the problem of being where I was helping the kids, but also getting close to kids, to offend, but I also feel for kids who are abused or treated badly by their parents. I suppose my idea of love is just totally wrong – cuddles isn't just any cuddles. That's what it started off as – a bit of caring – and, again, the big contradiction of my life.

I have a goddaughter and her parents still talk to me, obviously didn't like what I did, but they still talk to me OK. My goddaughter is 14 but I don't have any contact with her because she's got friends. I found my younger brother through Friends Reunited [the social networking website]. I'd been trying to find him for years. He was in the army. He came down to see me in August [2010] with his family, stayed in a hotel. We started to make amends, so I wanted to tell him face to face, but probation advised me to email before it went any further so I did that. He didn't want any more to do with me but he's not going tell my mum and dad. They wouldn't have known I was in prison as I had lost contact when I was in the air force.

[On being apprehended] It was the fact that it's me out, and I'm caught. I tried taking an overdose; I was taken out in an ambulance [from home]. In court I was instructed not to look at the audience, but you see it in the corner of your eye – there was a lot of hatred and looks, it was horrible. It's probably what I hated most, so why lie? I pleaded guilty: there was a couple of the things that I pleaded guilty to also but I wasn't sure about, but I just put my hands up to that anyway. There was certainly relief it was over [when sentence was passed]. I didn't know there was a course. I just expected to be locked up, key thrown away in a sense. I was expecting 14 years anyways, I was told to expect it, so it was a bit of relief that I only got eight, but it's a long time.

Yeah, I wasn't too keen on it [being separated in prison]. I didn't want to be. I mixed pretty well with most people. You don't really know each other's offence; it's never broadcast unless you see it on the news sort of thing. No, we never wanted to discuss it. On the course, it's different but the rule is anything you'd said on the course, it stayed on the course.

The time [in prison] was slow. Initially, I thought I wasn't getting out, because I did have a couple of suicidal thoughts, but that's when I used to do things for other prisoners, which helped me become looser myself. I got a bit of joy out of helping other people, gave me a sense of belonging in a sense. It was something to do, and there was a sense of trust from the officers, and I needed that, I needed people to, not respect me as such, but accept me for who I am. It was in prison that I came out [about being gay]. And the response, oh, it was amazing. I mean, there might be a couple of sly remarks behind my back, but most people just left me alone. I was happy, but I was just so surprised.

There was a bit of battle with one or two of the staff who called me a poof. But, no, nothing [hostility] like I expected, no. It's always helped, the fact I've been big anyway, but I never portrayed myself as the hard man or whatever, but some people would pick on others.

I spent time inside on education. I helped teach reading, and I did a couple of courses – English and computers – and then I did a little job, just cleaning. I was an orderly at the SOTP – making coffee and that for the groups, things like that – and again that's special because you're in among the staff, the psychologists, and you're actually making their tea without them worrying that you'd spit in it. (That shocked me; I didn't think prisoners would do that.)

I didn't want to come out [of prison]. The last actual night before I came out it was traumatic. I wanted to stay, to be honest; I didn't want to face the outside. I couldn't sleep, suicidal thoughts were there, and again, I mean, it was the self-talk, or I would have tried to. I knew the hostel where I was going but I needed to take a train there and I hadn't been on a train for 30 years. It was everyday things like that that caused the worry. And then, you see, you can be there for an hour, or two hours sometimes [waiting to be discharged]. Again, the anxiety is waiting, waiting, and in the end, I was there for about half an hour, and then it's 'Collect your stuff, take you to the gate, let you go, out you go, taxi's waiting for you, there's your tickets.' I went to the hostel and things weren't so bad at the start, in fact pretty good, but then I was recognised by my first victim's brother who was also there. I had no idea that he was in prison. So I moved to another hostel [in the town where I now live].

[*How did you learn about Circles?*] Probation officer visited me in prison and told me about it and advised me to join. He'd give me the address and advised me to write to [the regional co-ordinator], which I did.

[*What did you think about Circles at first?*] Again, rumours that I heard in prison: Circles are there but they're all ex-judges, they're all ex-coppers, they're only there to try and keep an eye on you, so if you mention anything to them they'll nick you straight back into prison. [The co-ordinator] killed that myth way back. He spoke to me more about what they teach, what they do. It was nerve-racking meeting the group the first time. I didn't know what to expect. In my mind, it was negative even if they were so what I needed. But I thought that they would still look down at me a little bit, but once I got to know them I realised that they're there for public safety as well as my own well-being, and the fact that they'd be honest with you about anything I did that came up. It crossed my mind as far as a couple were Quakers – I'm not really up on a religion – but I thought [sex offending] was always a no-no, with any form of religion, not to be not tolerated full stop, but punished. But when I came to talk to them I couldn't see anything in their eyes that was hatred or anything like that; they weren't doing it for glory. I prepared to tell them anything.

[*Did you fear anyone being judgemental?*] No, but I welcome it, in a sense, as a challenge, whereas before I would have run away. They spell it out. In the original [Circle] there were two volunteers who had to leave for personal reasons, and initially there was that fear of, 'Oh, they've left because of me.' Then they would explain why they'd had to leave and I just accepted it.

Yes, definitely, most definitely I look more ahead than I used to because I couldn't care less before, what I did. OK, it happened, I made a mistake, but now I try to eliminate any mistakes I can. If I still make a mistake then it's a fault but I tried, but I will not produce any more victims.

When I first started, I thought the volunteers'd pry. What are they up to? But I suddenly thought, 'Well, they wanna help, I want them to help, I wanna be able to go out, to eliminate any fear of reoffending if I can, there's no way I wanna reoffend.' People say, 'It's always in the [offender's] head and they're getting too close to that kid.' But the volunteers themselves, they're reassuring apart from anything else; they try and get me to blend in with other groups if I can. Yeah, reassurance that I'm doing the right thing, using self-talk, being able to share what I was doing on my courses, doing the wheel of life [a means of plotting one's life course and how events have occurred is also taught on the

SOTP] – I'm proud of. I took it to the volunteers. They were looking at it themselves as it can apply to anybody – all of your life; you see it in black and white: what you were like at the offence and what you're like now.

I need to be pushed. It's not that I'm not motivated really, but once I get going and I know they're [Circles] there for me, I've only got to say, 'I'm not too sure about this, could you help me?' and they're there. There's one [volunteer] – she's a little wise – and she took me on this walk that she does with her mother. It's like a march down the river and I was absolutely knackered. It was about a four-mile walk, but I enjoyed it; you know, I was out in the fresh air, talking about everyday things, with somebody my own age. It was just amazing, nobody's going to say about something, 'That's because you're a poof or you're looking at that kid.' There doesn't seem to be an atmosphere. I would like to be able to tell her anything.

I wouldn't have managed without them. The hostel staff were helpful but there's a limit to what they can offer. They take you out to groups, things like that, but there's no one-to-one, whereas with the Circles they're there, they're not doing it to get paid, it's something that they wanna do. [Without Circles] I think, to be honest, I would probably have committed suicide, because I wouldn't have been able to interact with adults properly. They've been supportive enough for me to get to know other people, being able to talk to them. I'm able to talk to neighbours now, whereas before I just kept my head down: the neighbours would say 'Hi' and I'd ignore them.

Prison was totally different, it's not real life. Anything you do in prison you can't practise in real life and that's what was great about the courses because I've been able to put it into practice. You come across a lot of self-talk, looking at your life, how to change your life.

As I tried to explain to [offenders], if [volunteers] were just retired prison officers and judges, it wouldn't work because nobody would be trusting in a Circle and staying with it, they just wouldn't. I mean, there's ups and downs with it – you're gonna get told off, as I do, but I respected it and I loved it.

[*How much do you know about the volunteers?*] I don't know what they do. I think one, she's got kids, but they don't say much about their lives. I know one of them's gay, which was a big help to me. He hasn't come out and told me, but he talks about his partner and his partner's name's is a man's, so… It helps knowing that there's somebody that I could turn to if I had any gay problems – I could actually talk to him about it if I've got any fears. He's so supportive, I mean he's telling me about a gay pub, but I don't wanna go to a pub because people there are going to get picked up for sex. I don't want that, I want to get to know more gay people and have a social relationship rather than a sexual one initially.

[*Have you thought of phoning a gay switchboard?*] If I don't know the person I'm talking to I'm a bit wary – you're lucky I'm talking to you. I think it was too raw. If it's gonna help, it's gonna help. The more I thought about my life, I think the better I understand it and that's what I liked about some of the groups, it's understanding myself. I mean a lot of the time I was so immature, it was unbelievable. I always wanted to be around younger people not necessarily for sex, but I think there was a control element. But now I've been able to be honest with people, I don't even look at control.

Things got out of hand, not being able to admit my sexuality, and it caused me to do things deviously. I think had I been able to express my sexuality as some brave people did, I think it'd have been a lot better. I'd have been able to grow up with my own age group, if you like.

[*But you still retain that sexual attraction for much younger people?*] Yeah, and I don't know where that stems from. I don't think I've really had a proper serious relationship with an adult. [If the right person came along] I'd be quite open about it and I would welcome it. But, as I said, I don't wanna go to these clubs and pubs where it's only about being there to just have sex.

[*Would you like to see your daughter again?*] It's in my blood. There's a bit of me wants to explain why I haven't been there for her but, knowing her mother, she'd have told her what I've done anyway, but I'd like, in some way, to make it up to her. Yeah, I've missed her very, very much. I mean, I haven't stopped thinking about her, wonder what she's up to, that sort of thing. Has she gone on school trips? Has she got friends?

I've got a future, but getting a job's difficult. A lot of it's because of the offence and you can see it in their eyes. It destroys the interview, they just don't wanna know.

If they don't ask, you don't have to tell them, which is why I want to get a heavy goods driving licence back, because most of that sort of job is OK. I don't want to be away too long because you get lonely, but I looked into that for the future. I think going back to trucking is possible, although I don't really want to because the roads are chaotic. But if I can get a job like that, a better flat than I'm in now (hopefully on the council lists), with maybe a few friends I could meet socially, not necessarily gay people.

I have a couple of friends now. I see my goddaughter's dad and he's 30-odd now and he's been down to see me. Again, he doesn't like what I've done but he's willing to give me the benefit, and neighbours, they're OK, they don't know about the offence, they don't know I'm gay yet but they're not hostile against gays. I will disclose to them, but I'll wait – I don't want to just blurt it out. Just making a casual remark can make as big a point and I'll just casually mention it. If it came up and they said, 'Are you a poof?' or something I'd say, 'Oh, yeah,' you know that sort of thing.

[*Where does your optimism come from?*] Don't know, but maybe, again, because the people out there believe in me, like the Circle. But I don't think I've ever been an optimist. Fifteen years ago, if we'd met, I was totally different – you'd have got all the lies, to be honest, I would have told you what you wanted to hear, made it up. For example, I would have told you I had been in the air force, had a pilot's licence – just trying to boost myself up – been around the world when I've only been in a couple of countries. I tried to make myself out as someone people want to know. Looking back at it, they wouldn't be friends, so it was in the prison that I decided, 'No more lies.'

It was like a new start. It was quite impulsive again, but I wanted people to know me as me. The prison talked to the solicitor and the police obviously, and the police actually thanked me for being honest [by pleading guilty] and telling me that I'd be saving the boys from having to appear in court. Things like that made it worthwhile in a sense. Nobody had actually spoken like that before and they did. People didn't really know me. So there's never been a true friendship, but now, as I say, I speak to somebody and I feel so happy that I don't have to make my life up.

George Davies: 'The future is now a day-to-day sort of thing'

George Davies is an unassuming man and his first words to me are to hope that I am better after a previously postponed meeting. Born in the north-east 57 years ago, his father was in the building trade and his mother was a housewife. He now lives in a remote village and we meet in a probation hostel not far from his home and where he lived after leaving prison. He pleaded guilty for taking, making and keeping indecent images and two counts of indecent assault. He received an indeterminate imprisonment for public protection sentence with a three-year tariff but successfully appealed against the IPP ('it gives you no hope') and finally served 18 months of his sentence. (It seems likely that the IPP was linked to the fantasy story, called The Rape of Sue, which had been found.) At the time of our meeting (October 2010), his licence had five months to run.

The offences were against his then 13½ year old niece (she is now aged over 16). After being made redundant, he went to live with one of his two brothers (he also has a sister) and his partner (his brother's wife had left during the period that George lived in the house). His niece had not been aware of the offences when they took place – George had secreted a camera in the bathroom and the two assaults, which he also filmed, happened while she slept. He says that his offences are the only ones which he has ever committed and that he had never had – or has now – any other sexual interest in children or young people. He admits that his relationships with women 'have never amounted to much' and this may be due to the lack of self-confidence to which he admits. His right side has been slightly paralysed since childhood, something of which he is conscious insofar as he says that had he not been disabled his life would have been different.

Before moving to live with his brother he had lived for many years in one of the Home Counties and had worked for almost the same period doing administrative work in the printing industry. At the time of our meeting, it seemed he had secured a voluntary job for two days a week with a nature conservation group (he had previously spent a year at one time as an attendant at one of the larger National Trust properties in the area). He had hopes that this might lead to the full-time, paid job which he wants. At this time, too, he had started the sex offender treatment programme and had been a core member of his Circle for ten months. George had carefully prepared notes in advance of our meeting, and occasionally he read from them.

My parents lavished a lot of time and effort to help me through the early part of my life [due to my disability]. My mother would take me to the local orthopaedic hospital, which was a round trip of about 50 miles, and she did this twice a week on public transport. My father was a practical person and devised an exercise bar in the garden that I could swing on to help me develop the strength in my right arm.

My parents were good, hard-working people and tried to instil in me and my two brothers and sister life's values. I had a good relationship with my siblings and when I moved to [the Home Counties], when I was 27, I would come back to the family home, which was now [near Manchester], on a regular basis. When my parents died I felt that a great void had opened up in my life. I would visit my siblings who now had their own homes and if I could help them out in any way I would. There was nothing in my background that explained what happened later [his offence].

The growth of my sexual attraction to my niece started quite innocently. I was holidaying at the public house my brother and his wife were managing at the time and one evening I broke my right arm quite badly. I was incapacitated for about 13 weeks and had to stay at the pub during this time, as I couldn't drive back home and wouldn't have been able to work or look after myself. My brother and his wife did a lot for me, but what really surprised me was how helpful my niece was – she was only about 11 years old at the time. She really went out of her way to help me and I became quite fond of her. After my illness I returned to work but was made redundant about a year later. I decided to move and my brother suggested that I should live with them. I had previously lent him a sum of money to buy a tenancy of a local public house.

My niece was getting older and developed into a lovely young woman, and my feelings for her strengthened. At this time also my brother's marriage hit the rocks, he had problems and his wife moved out of the pub. I got blamed for this, which I had got nothing to do with at all, and I got blamed for a lot of other things that I also had nothing to do with. I felt really low at the time and felt that I was getting old and was unloved, while my niece, on the other hand, was popular and well liked. I became obsessed with her and my feeling for her became warped and I started to fantasise about her, and this led to me committing the offences. At the time I knew that I was doing wrong, but I was driven by a strong force. I felt a very strong compulsion to do it, unfortunately. I think at the time because I was not in a relationship, I was feeling unloved, and what I was doing was giving me some sort of sexual excitement.

I consider that it was force of circumstances: I mean, I'd lived on my own basically for 20-odd years and I was thrust back into a family atmosphere and… As I say, I think it was because of the caring nature as well. I'd become fond of her and then that fondness had taken a sort of warped turn, as it were.

[*But why did you think it expressed itself in a sexual way?*] I don't know. I mean, I'd moved to an area where I didn't have any friends, there wasn't any sort of place to sort of really meet anybody, and, as I said, she was maturing at the time and I had got feelings for her, and those feelings became warped, I'm afraid. I didn't believe she was a victim because this was done covertly, so I thought she didn't know, she wasn't aware of it.

How did I justify it? Well, as I said, because nobody knew what I was doing, I thought – I honestly thought – I wasn't hurting anybody at the time. I mean since doing the sex offenders' course obviously I realise differently from that. It wasn't the norm, no, I appreciate that, but, as I say, at the time I was lonely, no self-esteem, you know, and consequently I went down the wrong path.

She found a video camera and the tape was still in it. I don't know [how she reacted] – she passed it on to my brother's girlfriend and I was arrested about a week later. My brother and his girlfriend, they sort of distanced themselves from me during this time, didn't say a lot to me really, which is understandable. I stayed there. It lasted about a week [until his arrest]. Not my niece, though: she lived with her mother, she would visit the pub from time to time; she wasn't living there permanently.

I wish it hadn't happened, I obviously do – the hurt I've caused these people…the family, friends, et cetera, and, obviously, the victim. As part of the [SOTP] course we've looked at films of people talking about their experience of being the victim and it's harrowing, it really is, and to think that my niece is going through something like that is, you know…really, really, it hurts me.

It was obviously a dark side of me, but it was a blip in my life. I've done many good things in my life, you know, helped people and what not. If somebody comes up to me and says can you do such and such, I think about it and if I can, I will. It's difficult to sort of fathom really. It was a build-up of things. I might have had some sort of a nervous breakdown or something, I don't know, but it certainly wasn't me, as far as I know myself, it was just, yeah, it was a different person completely.

[Do you think that had an opportunity arisen it could have gone further?] That I don't know, and in some respects I'm grateful I was arrested at the time, because I think that brought it to a halt as it were, so I don't know, I honestly don't know. I mean, when you're doing it, you say, 'Oh, I'm gonna stop now,' and then you say, 'No, I'll carry on a little bit longer.' It could quite possibly have done, and that would have been absolutely horrible if something like that would have happened.

Because of the nature of my crimes and because of my lack of friends, I couldn't discuss it with anyone and I also believe that I wouldn't have had the courage to do that. When I was committing the offences

I believed that because no one was aware, including my victim, that I wasn't hurting anyone. I now know that this is far from the truth.

I have never had an attraction for children. No, as I said, I think basically it was because my niece, during the broken arm period of my life, was really helpful – you know, she really went out of her way to help, to look after me when she was only 11 at the time, which I found quite charming.

I'd had relationships with women, but they'd never amounted to much really, if I said truthfully. I think I did find it easier to speak to younger people than people of my own age. I always lacked the confidence, I think, to speak to people of my own age, and because of my disability as well I was always quite self-conscious.

No, I don't [fear I would reoffend]. I mean I lost a hell of a lot: I lost friends, family, I had to sell my house, and what with this that and the other, you know, I've lost quite a lot, and I don't want to go down that path again… I'm 95 per cent certain I wouldn't reoffend, but I think the SOTP course does help.

[*If you were near, say, a school and you saw girls of 11, 12, 13 – would you think that they were sexually attractive?*] No. No, as I say, I think it was because of the sort of relationship I had with being fairly close to my niece – I think that that's what's put me on that track, you know.

When I was told I could expect a prison sentence I was absolutely petrified at the prospect. I was interned at [prison] during my remand period and I felt very threatened. I was there for a period of six weeks. After my trial at Mold Crown Court I was transferred to [prison] and placed on the vulnerable persons' wing. I didn't feel threatened there and after a short while I found myself finding my feet. I began to settle into life in prison and I know prison is a punishment but I also expected some rehabilitation work, which did not materialise, possibly because I was appealing the IPP part of my sentence which took about seven months. Also because there was a shortage of spaces in prison for the courses that would be relevant to me, and because my prison term was only 18 months, I presume that they thought it would be better if I did the courses upon my release. I felt guilty and didn't contact my family for about six months during this period and I had to steel myself to make that first phone call. I found the structure of prison very regimented, with timings to do certain things like library visits and gym visits, et cetera. The only thing I gained – and I am grateful for that – was passing my ECDL [European Computer Driving Licence] parts 1 and 2, and also gaining an art certificate. Prison was a deterrent for me but I am not sure about the rehabilitation side.

I was on the vulnerable prisoners' wing – not all sex offenders, about 50:50 – but the prison officers they were very, very good. Never felt threatened at all, and some of the other inmates were quite friendly, and we had a carer – his wasn't a sex offence – on the wing, and he'd given me quite a lot of help when I first arrived there, you know. He lives up the road now. He's got a little bungalow and I see him occasionally, keep in touch with him. A very, very good person.

I haven't spoken to my brother [father of the victim] directly since the offence, well, since I was arrested. He and his wife had been round to see my other brother and sister. They were absolutely dumb… I mean, first of all, when they went round there and said, 'We've got some bad news about George,' they thought I'd passed away, but I think they were even more astounded as to what I'd done, which is understandable. My sister, being a mother herself, couldn't come to terms with it; in fact, I think she was revolted by it. I had about four visits from [my brother] Brian and my sister, but the first time she didn't come, you know, she couldn't come, she was still upset and in shock.

The whole family had a meeting and asked that when I came out I would not live in their areas or visit them, so, therefore, I'm, you know, self-banned from [the areas near Manchester]. I haven't seen them since I left prison, apart from Brian; he's been down to the flat I've got now. He's been a great support and sorted out things like financial matters when I was in prison. I speak to him regularly on the phone. His wife doesn't agree with him. She won't speak to me; I mean, she will speak to me, but it's quite terse.

I've written to my sister a few times since leaving prison and received a card last Christmas [2009], but all other communications have gone unanswered. So Brian's the only one, apart from an aunty who supported me while I was in prison, writing to me on a regular basis, trying to keep my spirits up. She is 87 years old and when I came out of prison, she said she wasn't going to write any more, but we could communicate by phone, which we've done. I don't think anybody in their right mind could accept what I've done.

Friends? I don't make friends that easily. I had a lot of friends from my school days – this is going back, like 40, 50 years sort of thing – but we kept in touch and we used to meet up quite regularly, even when most of them still live [near Manchester], but even when we sort of moved away from one another – I mean one of them was in France – we'd still meet up, and that was good but… They've had mixed reactions to my crimes and I don't blame them: if the boot was on the other foot, I would've reacted the same way.

I'd just come out of prison and was stationed here, and one of my friends had my brother's number and he got my number, and they rang me because one of my friends had passed away – very sad, hell of a nice chap – and they're saying did I want to go to the funeral. I hadn't got my transport then and because of the nature of the offence I was only allowed out a couple of hours a day in the first weeks [imposed as a condition of residence in the hostel] anyway, so I couldn't have really got to the [funeral] and back. I also thought that if I went up there I would sort of detract from his funeral, everybody'd be asking me questions and I didn't think that would be right in the sort of circumstances, so I declined. Anyway, the friend who rang me, I told him I'd been in prison, I didn't go into the nature of it, but he said, 'When you're ready, you know, come up and we'll have a chat.' He's quite an understanding chap, but I haven't yet because I don't like talking about it really.

I was a bit concerned when I left prison, fearing that I would be on my own with little or no support which could possibly lead back into a path of reoffending. This has not been the case as I have received a lot of support from many bodies: probation, PPU [Public Protection Unit] and, not least of all, my Circles group. The Circle members have not judged me, and I find it easy to speak to them about problems that occur in my life. They possess a wealth of knowledge, which has been beneficial to me. I feel that if I have a problem in between meetings there is always someone there to help me. Probation and PPU are also there to help me not reoffend, although their methods are a bit more structured. I think that all the organisations complement each other and I have been pleasantly surprised by all the help I've received, I feel that it's gone a long way to helping me through this period and stop me from reoffending.

With Circles, I was lucky really because I was put here [in the hostel where we meet] and I was speaking to the main staff about fearing that I would be on my own, little help and whatever, and they said, 'We've got a lady here who's the sort of manager [co-ordinator] of the [regional] branch of Circles: would you like us to get you in touch with them?' And I said, yes.

It was explained to me and I felt it was good, I felt if they can be bothered to talk to me, and show me support – and that is what I wanted – it was all well and good. I'm very grateful. Yes, initially, I had some anxiety but they haven't judged me, and, basically, they've taken me for who I am, you know. I mean it was a one-off period in my life. I've done plenty of good things in my life, so they've tried to help me through this period. Yes, good things, but that offence nullified everything.

[*I wouldn't say it nullified everything but it gave you a label – the sex offender – so how did you think you'd stop the label hiding who you are?*] I don't think I ever will, you know. I mean, I feel guilty if I'm walking down the street and I'm not supposed to speak to young people, so if I see a young person I try and avoid them. I'm always looking over my shoulder; it is difficult. I can only hope that as time goes by things will get easier.

Yeah, it's worrying [that living in so small an area the facts may get out]. Basically, when I left prison I didn't want to go back to the [the area where he comes from]. But the PPU and probation said that no, they couldn't accept me in this area because I hadn't got any sort of connections here, and as the offence was committed in [area] that's where I'd have to go back to, because I was under [area] probation. Otherwise, I would have fought shy of going that direction, but saying that, you know, I'm there now and no problems as such at the moment.

Without Circles, I wouldn't have had anybody to talk to. I mean, you've got probation and you've got PPU, but I never feel relaxed with them, but I feel relaxed with the Circle members. I don't know why… because…I find their questions quite searching, you know, and I think to myself they believe I've changed, but I can understand that they might not do. Well, they feel relaxed with me. There's three of them, yet on occasions I've met with only one of them, so they obviously can't consider me much of a threat, and I find that refreshing. I did mention that to them at one of the meetings. [One of the volunteers] said, 'No, we don't consider you a threat. We're quite happy to meet with you on a one-to-one basis,' so that was good, I thought.

I was lacking in confidence, really lacking in confidence, and I think they've boosted that part of my life. I wouldn't say I'm the most confident person at the moment at all, but I'm definitely better than what I was, so they've instilled that in me, you know – be more confident.

Obviously, the offence has made me feel bad about myself and given me this lack of confidence, but also I think that part of this offence could also be down to me being that I am disabled. I think if I hadn't been disabled my life would have been probably totally different.

[*Why should three people sitting in a room with you increase your self-confidence?*] Because they are prepared to talk to me and they talk to me about all sorts of subjects, not just about, you know, the sexual nature of things. They've given me help when I need it, things like pointing me in the right direction. They were the first ones to mention about voluntary work and where to try. They put me in touch with somebody and, hopefully, things will grow from there. And there's practical things, like when my car had been in a garage for 12 months when I was prison. [The regional Circles co-ordinator] said she'd run me. PPU and probation might be a bit more structured, but, with Circles, it's more to do with my spirit, I dare say: they make my spirit feel good.

So, yes, I do feel a bit more reassured now. I felt very bad about what I'd done, and not to sort of decry that sort of thing, but I am feeling a bit better now in myself anyway. I know I've done wrong, but I feel I can live with myself now. At one point I was depressed, I wasn't suicidal, no, but I just felt pain all the time.

I don't know how my future will unfold, but I think it will be better with the help I have received from the group. So I remain with a positive outlook. I always, you know, I think to myself…even though this will always be with me, I don't want to dwell too much on it. The facilitators [of the SOTP] say, 'We don't want you to be thinking about this one hundred per cent of the time because that's doing you no good, no good at all.'

It's a day-by-day sort of thing, isn't it? No, it's not always been like that. I was looking far ahead a few years ago perhaps, but not any more, no. Well, you never know what's round the corner do you, now? Prior to the offence I had got very little fear of anything, but now I'm always sort of on tenterhooks because, as you've said, there's a possibility that it might come out, so I try to avoid situations where that might happen.

THE VOLUNTEERS' STORIES

Laurence Clark: 'We're all capable of anything given certain circumstances'

Laurence Clark says: 'I've done everything upside down and the wrong way round. I did everything ten years later than everyone else.' He is a friendly, articulate man, who often dots his story with amusing asides. His father was an insurance salesman who, in his 40s, became, with his mother, a restaurateur. His parents, he says, were 'quite bohemian', a non-conformist quality which their son seems to have inherited. He has a half brother, but says that he had 'quite a lonely childhood'. He was sent to boarding school at the age of seven. Expelled from school when he was 17, he spent a year at the University of Grenoble, France, and then worked in an advertising agency, as a junior reporter on the Cambridge Evening News, and as a trainee buyer at Selfridges. Moving to Shropshire, he signed on the dole and as a result got a job as an assistant teacher in a school for what were then called maladjusted children. He took to teaching and entered teacher training college and then gained a 2:1 in English Literature at Exeter College, Oxford (where a college contemporary was Martin Amis). After a short spell working in the state sector, he bought a prep school which he ran for 33 years, an irony he likes given his expulsion – 'a poacher turned gamekeeper'. A member of about ten Circles and, with the one-to-one mentoring he also does through Circles, he reckons he has worked with about 20 ex-offenders, with whom about ten he still retains contact. He lives with his partner Jacque and has two adult daughters. Our meeting takes place in his large, book-filled, comfortable house in a village in Buckinghamshire.

Maybe because I was expelled from school, I've always liked rogues and one reason perhaps I became a prison visitor. What gave me a buzz about teaching was identifying and unlocking the potential in children, and when I was deciding that I'd retire I wanted something that tapped into that and so I applied to become a prison visitor at Grendon Underwood [a unique prison which offers serious offenders therapeutic care].

The first person I was to see was Alan, a sex offender. I must admit that I wondered what I'd let myself in for. After all, prison visitors are supposed to befriend. I thought perhaps I wouldn't be able to do that. I think, too, that I expected him to be rather creepy. The reality was very different. From the moment I first met Alan I liked him – he was a big chap and very jolly. I said to him, 'Look, there's no point in our discussing trivial things. If we are going to have a meaningful relationship, I need you to tell me your story,' and he said, 'Are you sure?', but I told him that it was important to me that he did. He had had a terrible upbringing. His mother had used him from the ages of five to 12 to sexually gratify herself every night. I simply couldn't imagine the trauma that something like that had on a young child. He'd gone on to abuse two boys. At the end of his story, I told him that I was amazed, given his childhood, that he hadn't done something far worse. He rounded on me, saying that was no excuse – lots of people had terrible childhoods but they didn't go on to abuse children.

What impressed me about Alan was that he wasn't disposed to blame anyone else for what had happened. He and only he was responsible for what he'd done. He made it clear to me that he would do whatever it took never to reoffend. He said that he didn't expect that I would want to see him again after what he'd told me but I said that I would come again. He looked sceptical but thanked me profusely for letting him tell me his story. I found his gratitude embarrassing. When I saw him I said, 'There is one thing that gets up my nose about you – and that's your fucking gratitude.' I said I wanted the relationship between us to be one of equality. He looked amazed because, as he said, no one had ever said that to him before. 'When you talk to me I don't feel that you're looking at the label that's on my forehead,' he said 'but you're looking at me as a person.'

Him being at Grendon meant he went through a very painful experience – he had literally been in hell – but it brought about great change in him. I admired his courage and determination in facing his demons. It was hellishly difficult for him, but he stuck with it through everything, so determined was he to put offending behind him once and for all.

One day I said to Alan that I was very worried about him when he left. I said, 'You're OK in Grendon but when you get out, how will you manage? You could easily slide back into reoffending.' He said that wasn't going to let that happen because he had come across this outfit called Circles and he gave me all sorts of bumpf about it and I started to think that that was something that I could get involved in.

I went to see him six months later just before he was due to be released and he said to me, 'When you came to see me I felt like a piece of shit at the bottom of a dark well, but I am not there any more and you've been part of that process.' The next morning I had a call from the chaplain. 'Sad news,' he said. 'Alan had a heart attack in the night and died.' Something in me told me that he knew that that was our last meeting and that's why he had said what he'd said. I was really moved by it and, in a way, it was the inspiration and impulse for me to join Circles and I went on the first training course nine years ago.

For my last three years as a head teacher I was in a Circle so I had to decide whether to keep that a secret or let it be known. I decided on the latter. Many parents did ask me about it, and I was very encouraged by their reaction when I explained it. Mostly the public don't understand. They think of the predatory sex offender as portrayed in the media, but actually most sex offenders are much more mundane. Most offend within the family or with friends. It's an addiction, but, like any addiction, where there's a will, it can be managed and the risk can be avoided. I got very positive reactions from all my school parents once I had explained this, which I found very heartening.

Jacque said, 'Look, I really don't want to know about this. I've got no problem with you doing it at all, but I don't want any sex offenders ringing us or coming home.' I said not to worry about that: the policy is that they don't know our home address, they don't know our telephone numbers, they don't know anything. (Ironically, she's rather taken to another man I visited in prison, a lifer, a convicted murderer.) My daughters are very relaxed about it.

Funnily enough, I asked the guy who was doing some plumbing work for us when he could come again and when he said the week, I said that wouldn't be around as I was going to Holland. When he asked why, I said it was about this work I do on the rehabilitation of offenders. He wanted to know what that was about and I explained to him about Circles and he was absolutely fascinated. I find if people can see that what you're trying to do is actually prevent further offending, then they seem to be pretty relaxed about it.

The experience that I had with Alan, though I didn't realise it at the time, was exactly what happens in a Circle: the process that takes place involves a man who has lived, literally, in hell, moving out of that place and finding he is more than the total sum of his offences and becoming a reconstructed human being – that's the process that we obviously hoped to reproduce in Circles, and I have seen it a few times since.

I thought, you know, it seems like such a small thing that I'm doing here but actually it's something absolutely vital, because I suppose the system, not intentionally, is by and large, very judgemental. Obviously, it's the job of the police, probation and the prison service, and you are identified solely by your offence, whereas I think a prison visitor or the volunteers in a Circle are not actually there to be judgemental; they're interested in human beings. We don't label. For us they are not solely sex offenders. They are men who have committed sexual offences. There is a difference. We abhor the offences but we respect the offender. That's a revelation to the offender.

When we first meet in a Circle with core members, generally speaking there's a good degree of suspicion on the part of the core member, that we are just a kind of an adjunct of the system that's always judged them and labelled them. They'll ask with incredulity, 'What are you're doing here? Are you being paid?' 'No,' we say. 'Well, why are you doing it?' So we say, 'Well, for two reasons. One is we want to prevent further victims being created and, second, we want to see if we can help you to change your life,' and they find that quite difficult to come to terms with for a while. The more they talk and tell us things about themselves, and the more we relentlessly go back every week and are not put off by whatever they tell us, eventually the trust gets built up and that is quite extraordinary and very empowering. The offender begins to experience a hitherto unknown self-respect. That's the real magic of Circles really – that relationship of trust that grows up: they discover we don't have a hidden agenda.

There's a contract: we say, 'Look, if we think you're engaging in risky behaviour, we will report that – that's the deal. Our purpose is "No more victims" and we hope to achieve that by helping you to find strategies to enable you to lead a risk-free life, and to engage with the community and the adult world in a responsible way, but if we fail to do that and you start to drift back to your old patterns then we'll shop you. That's the deal – no more victims one way or another.'

Because of the relationship they'll tell us things in a Circle that they've never told anybody, and that's incredibly liberating for them, because all sorts of stuff is bottled up that's been stewing for years, and it'll come out. We treat anything they tell us as confidential, unless it constitutes a risk.

There is kind of process that seems to take place in a Circle. At first the core member is facing backwards towards their offending or their obsessions, or whatever it is, and we get that out because it has to come out. It has to be aired and into the open. Then we concentrate on getting the core member to face the future. And then there is a point, a pivotal point in the Circle, and the member can start moving forward and build a new life.

I remember one Circle where that wasn't happening, and we were becoming very frustrated. However, the core member let slip one day that he actually wrote a diary, and I suggested to the Circle that reading this diary might be the key to unlocking the problem of his obsession with this little girl. [The Circle volunteers] agreed that I should ask him and report back to the Circle. So I read it and it was horrid, but an important and significant issue did emerge, namely that his own children were really shut out of his life. They were just procurers [for their friends] and he seemed to have little love or time for them.

We were able to point this out to him and he was shocked. He hadn't realised how sidelined his children had become. He said, 'Well, obviously they don't like the fact that I offended against one of their friends.' We pointed out that the diary barely mentioned them other than as bit players, so obsessed was he with their friends. He didn't seem to have much interest in them at all. He looked actually really shocked. We asked him, 'Do you love them?' 'Oh yeah, of course I love them,' he said. We pointed out that it didn't come across that way. We suggested that he remove from his wall a photograph of his victim. 'If you've got this girl here all the time you're feeding your obsession; just take it down and throw it away.' He said that he couldn't do that. We said, 'OK, well, look, take it down and put it in a drawer then, but just don't have it up in front of you all the time.' He said he'd think about it, but when I next went to visit him, he had actually taken it down, and he'd put photographs of his own girls up on the wall. I said, 'Well done, that's fantastic,' but he said that something else had happened which had had a profound effect on him. He had rung his eldest daughter, and told her that he'd taken the picture of [the victim] down, and actually put their pictures up in its place. He said there was a long silence on the other end of the phone, and then he said, 'I could hear my daughter sobbing at the other end of the phone, and I said, "What's the matter, what's the matter?" and she said; "Dad, if you could see my face, I've got the biggest smile you could imagine."'

And, then, we volunteers invited him and his daughters out to a meal. In the middle of the meal one of them said, 'I'm so happy,' and when I asked why, she said, 'We've got our dad back,' and that, really, really turned him. He forged huge links with his family and his children, and it has been the making of him in many ways, and I think he's a changed man.

Volunteers in a Circle are very much a team. At the end of a Circle meeting, we'll have a chat about things and that's the time when we will share our insights or our misgivings, or we'll identify the problem areas that need to be addressed and what should we do in order to sort of deal with that. We'll then go back to the core member at the beginning of the next meeting – and this is about trust, which is so important – and say that we had a discussion afterwards and tell him what we discussed, and what we thought, and the insights we had, and where we think we should go next. It's important he doesn't feel he is being talked about behind his back and that full trust is maintained.

Some volunteers need lots of support if they're going through a difficult patch, For example, there was a young woman in one Circle who let on to us that she had herself been abused by her father all the way through her childhood and it had never really come out and she'd never really resolved it. We asked why she was volunteering and she said, 'I just want to help to reduce offending behaviour so that what happened to me doesn't happen to other people but I don't know if I'm going to be able to do it.' Then when we met the core member at the end of that meeting she said; 'I don't think I can do this, I don't like this bloke. He's really creepy; I just don't think I can hack it.' We said, 'Look, if you can't, you can't; don't worry about it.' Actually the guy wasn't creepy at all; she was obviously just projecting her own experience. But we said that if she did want to stick with it, we would be there for her, and she not only stuck with it, but what was rather interesting was that she and the core member actually formed quite a close relationship with one another, so much so that following a Christmas meal with this guy, she gave him a huge hug and said, 'Happy Christmas and thank you.' He just burst into tears and ran off.

I asked him later what it was like for him when she did that, and he said, 'I know she was abused all the way through her childhood, and it was like her saying to me, "Welcome back to the human race."' It was extraordinarily powerful, and he said, 'I learnt so much from her about what it's like for a victim,' and she said later that she'd learnt a lot from him about how it is for an abuser, so there was a real mutual healing going on there.

I think I've become maybe a little less naïve [over the years]. You do get jerked around if you're not careful. I know the old cliché about sex offenders is that they are really manipulative. That was one of the statements I objected to on our first training course, and I ended up saying, 'Well, who isn't? We're all manipulative. They're manipulative to those ends, and we're manipulative in other ways.' It's part of the human condition. I'm less trusting, perhaps, than I was, and so I'm asking more questions, digging a bit deeper, I think, than I did originally. Given the nature of offending and the deep shame and self-disgust offenders feel, it is not surprising that that they are sometimes evasive. These things are difficult to face.

From a very young age – I don't know quite when – it seemed to me that we're all capable of anything given certain circumstances, so I've never found it easy to be judgemental of my fellow human beings, because it seems to me we're all very flawed, given childhood experiences, or other experiences, or whatever. Because, in theory, they are pillars of the community, head teachers get asked to become magistrates. I was asked but I couldn't do it. You would look at the man in the dock, 'There but for the grace of God.' I didn't know what that man's life has been like, I don't know what's led up to him doing what he did. I just cannot feel comfortable making a judgement on him. OK, it has to be done, but it's just not me. I just look at anybody I meet in prison, or anywhere really, as being, you know, sort of flawed like me really. Some of us are unfortunately flawed in that we break laws, but I also think from that experience with Alan and others since that actually you can turn that round. It really is possible. So many people are in awful, hellish places that they can't escape from unless somebody offers them a helping hand.

I don't think I've ever been repelled: I guess that might be to do with being a head teacher. One of my senior teachers said to me, 'How the hell do you put up with some of these parents?' I said, 'You know how I do it? I learnt to do this very early on – I regard them as there to entertain me. I regard them as a sort of cavalcade of grotesques, who are there in some sort of vaudeville capacity for me, and the more bizarre and odd and gross they come across, the more entertaining I find it.' I suppose it's a protective thing, because if you let stuff in like that, you'd just be destroyed in no time. In a way, I feel outside it and I'm looking in on it. And I don't feel separate or apart from people. I think I'm probably as grotesque.

I think detachment is important for a Circles' volunteer. I don't think you can bleed, you know. In my very first Circle there was a very bright girl who had also been abused by her uncle when she was a kid, and she kept saying things to the core member, 'Look I've got a lot invested in you, you've got to succeed,' and I thought, 'Ah, no, you can't go there.

This is not about you.' It was a disastrous Circle, our first one, and it was a real learning curve. We were middle class, strong personalities, haranguing the core member, and arguing with each other. The Circle became about us and not about him. To her credit, she said, 'I've never resolved the abuse that I suffered and, consequently, I can't work on a Circle. I have to go off and sort it out for myself, because I can't do this projection.' So, yes, you've just got to have that detachment. We learnt a lot from that Circle about the importance of matching volunteers with one another and then the core member. The right balance is really important.

I don't bring all this home and worry about it. I think being a teacher helps you in a way, because, having done that for so many years, I learnt to put my professional concerns on one side when I come home, but sometimes I do get…sometimes it's heavy and then Jacque will sometimes say to me, 'You obviously had a pretty heavy session,' so I'll say, 'Wasn't really,' but she points out to me that I'm very heavy and quiet. I think it happens less in a Circle funnily enough because we support one another, but I do a lot of mentoring as well, one-to-one mentoring [through Circles]. That can be quite tough because you can't chat with your fellow volunteers because there aren't any, so you do a lot more chatting with your [Circles] co-ordinator, but you can't quite let off steam in the same way after the Circle's over. That's when sometimes it does get quite heavy. It can be quite difficult.

It just goes eventually; it'll just sort of fade away. I might ring up my co-ordinator. Talking it through is the way to get it off your chest. It's rather like when something's going round and round in your head, and sometimes it's writing it down that just gets it out there and you can let it go. I don't talk it through with Jacque: she doesn't really want to know, and, anyway, it's confidential so I couldn't tell her everything.

I think you're feeling your way all the time in a Circle, aren't you? One of the things I absolutely hate, that I hate in myself, as well as I hate in anybody, is a failure to realise our potential, and that's the big buzz I got from being a teacher: unlocking that. Somebody actually believes, 'This is where I am: I'm in a safe place and this is where I stay. I've got these walls around me; I'm not going beyond those walls.' As a teacher what I loved was encouraging the children to knock the wall down and saying, 'Come on, let's go on the other side of that wall and see what we can see.' And when they get there, they find it's not so frightening after all. Then you actually see someone absolutely flowering, it's such a buzz.

With offenders it's the same because they've always lived in this particular place and they've never felt anything else was possible for them. But you cannot work with somebody who doesn't want to go there, and there are some who can, who can want it really, really badly, but actually, in the end, just can't make it on their own. They just find it very, very tough, too tough, but with support and encouragement of a Circle, they find the courage and strength to achieve it.

There was one guy [in a Circle] who definitely wanted to address the problem but, in the end, he got recalled [to prison as he had been released on licence] after he had followed a boy. He came back onto the Circle again on release and what had happened was quite a salutary experience for him. Since then he's got his own place and seems to be doing quite well. But he had an horrendous childhood – he was part of a paedophile ring as a child and saw all sorts of ghastly things – and you thought this guy's so damaged he's never going to be different but he seems, touch wood, so far to have managed it. So it's about determination and it does involve enormous courage and the willingness to face a lot of pain, and go to very painful places in order to really come to terms with it and address it. Not everyone can do that.

It's a strange relationship [between volunteers and core members] in a way. We're very conscious that what we mustn't do is make that person dependent on us. In other words, they have to develop their own strength and their own independence, so at the same time as being really supportive, we have to sort of push them towards doing it for themselves. If we've got to that point in a Circle where that person is beginning to take off, or take wing, and getting involved with this, that and the other, I suppose it's a bit like – maybe this is not a very good analogy – when you're a parent and your kids leave home. You kind of accept that's fine, they can always ring up (usually for money!) but I think you recognise as a parent that you've done your bit and it's up to them to make their own way from that point. So you have a responsibility, as a parent, to be protective and steer them this way and that, but there is a point when you just sort of say goodbye, but you're always on the end of a phone if they need reassurance or to talk things through.

When we first started, the intention was that a Circle would last a year and that would be that, but, of course, it doesn't work like that really. You have worked with that person and in a pretty intimate way, and so consequently there is a link and there always will be a link, and if it needs to be used then it's there, that communication is there. That's the message, I suppose, that we always give our core members: 'If you need to contact us, you know what the number is, you know if you want to talk something through or something's come up that you need some help with, then let us know,' and they do from time to time.

When I look back on my life, I find an amazing pattern, situations that I have learnt from. Sometimes I say to offenders, 'What can you learn from your experiences?' If you don't address your weaknesses, then they repeat themselves. Life teaches you that difficult situations are there to be addressed, and are there for a reason. If you duck them, then the problem will always be with you.

We are all in this together. I have had a very lucky life and think that I should put myself out to help others who have not been so lucky. This is not virtuous; it just seems to me the obvious thing to do.

Elizabeth Cowie: 'Offenders are just people, aren't they?'

Elizabeth Cowie* is a softly spoken, thoughtful woman. She is a Quaker who hardly answers a question without first reflecting long on the answer. But at the end of the interview, she says of our discussion, with a self-deprecating smile, 'That wasn't me', and points to what she regards as the slightly intimidating presence of the microphone. She first heard about Circles when she was attending a national Quaker meeting in London. Immediately encouraged, it was not until some years later, though, that she had the chance to volunteer, when Circles came to her northern county. A former nurse, she has a commitment, in retirement, to voluntary work, all of which, she says, is about people. However, it was when she took part in her Circle training that she came to think more about her own abuse as a child, but more than that it was something she had never disclosed – at that point – even to her husband. Both are Circle members. They have children and grandchildren.

Friends had confided in me for several years about several cases of sex offending and I came across others when working. My daughter, as another example, came up against cases of sex offending and wanted advice about how she could help the person affected by the abuse. There was also something else at work that alerted me to it. I was very shocked because I suddenly realised how you can't identify sex

---

* Elizabeth Cowie is a pseudonym.

offenders. Where I worked one of the doctors had propositioned a young boy in public toilets in a town not far away, and he'd arranged to meet him later in the day. The young lad told someone, the police were there and they caught him. He'd dealt with small children, and he'd been given complete trust which you expect with a family doctor. He was a very well-respected person. I thought, yes, it could be anyone and…

When I was a child I was abused by somebody who was apparently respectable – that was a horrible shock. I couldn't come to terms with it until I joined the Circle and then I actually said something about it to my husband and he was, in turn, surprised and upset. I never told anyone because it was such a dreadful thing and you feel you might not be believed. I know that the victim feels that they're to blame in some way and they feel guilty and, and it was something, particularly at the time I grew up, that no one spoke about. You go back to it over and over again during your life, not constantly, but it's there, I think it sort of lurks there. I'm very concerned about the victims because I know what it can do.

When I came to the Circle, it meant that I could actually verbalise what had happened. I don't think it was the reason for joining. My main feeling was that these people [offenders] were coming out of prison and had no one, and I think that must be the most appalling position to be in. You can't imagine what it's like to come out of prison and to be so hated and know that really you have reached a point in your life where you can't go back and undo what's been done. There's no way forward, they're stuck in limbo and that's really the reason, I think, for me [being a Circles volunteer].

[And your Quaker faith, that's obviously something to do with it?] I think so, yes, yes. We are told there's something of God in everyone, and you can't just write people off for what they've done and also what has happened to them in their past has very often caused them to offend, I think, or, at least, didn't help them. Very often they have had no love, no contact with parents. There's been no example set of what we think of as a good life, a secure family unit, and they've been deprived of all sorts of things. Of course, we all have free will and maybe they haven't been taught where the barriers are, as we were. With children, you teach what is right and what is wrong and you build up this framework inside you and maybe they've never had that.

[You had your own experience, people told you things and you had this knowledge of the doctor, but what was the difference in actually having an offender sit with you every week for an hour, and talk?] It deepened it. Also, even after a year of doing Circles, which isn't very long, it's very difficult to see what is going on inside their minds and sometimes you feel as though there's another layer underneath which you simply can't tap into and sometimes you feel they're running rings around you, and other days you get quite attached to them. Well, in fact, you get to like them as people, but you know that you can't let that go too far because underneath all this, you think, 'I have no idea what's going on in their mind.'

[*So one of the challenges of being a volunteer is to keep a distance, be objective?*] Yes, certainly, and very often we do sit the core member in different places so that we can each get a different view of his face to see how he's interacting with us. Sometimes we'll sit him so the light's shining on him, which is very cruel, but you do see subtle variations in colour and facial expression.

Our first [core member] was totally different from the second one. I think the first one wasn't as deep as the second one and, I don't know…it was a very different relationship. We were all very sad when he decided not to continue because it was a quite jokey, fun sort of relationship and you felt as though you were getting to him. It was heartbreaking. I think the whole Circle felt we'd failed.

What happened was that he had formed an attachment to somebody in (I'll call it) a position of authority and he wanted to invite her out. We didn't know about this until it had reached the point he was going to ask her out. We talked it through with him but it was quite obvious that he was determined to go ahead with it. It was obvious that she might not want to know. He asked her and she took it the wrong way and all the alarms were set off and he saw this as an enormous rejection. While this could happen with anybody, he felt a loss of face and he never came back to Circles. I did see him in the street later on – but I was in a car so I couldn't talk to him – however, he looked quite confident.

Because we were a group we could talk about what happened and say how we felt. Another core member came to our Circle so we were distracted. If there had not been another core member for a few weeks it would have been a bit demoralising because we did feel as though we were working with him and making progress – and suddenly he was gone.

You have to be sensible about it, but we always talk about the first core member and I think we all got quite, not so much attached, as quite fond of him and protective really. Then, suddenly, he was out on his own. Having tried to form a relationship he hadn't got that to fall back on, so we don't know what happened. I always hope I'll bump into him and ask him.

With the second core member, he's two people – it's a much deeper relationship. Actually, on one occasion it made me very angry, and it wasn't something I'd really expected. I was really cross one day and said, 'I don't hate him, I hate what he's doing with us,' and that's when it becomes difficult. I felt that he was manipulating us, hiding things from us and I thought he wasn't on our wavelength. But, on the other hand, if I was in his situation I wonder whether I would be hiding things and being frightened of exposing myself.

[*If there are two people in the core member, so to speak, what does that say about your understanding of who a person is?*] I think two of my other volunteers are quite cynical, which is a very good balance actually in a Circle – that works very well. Two of us probably want to like him as a person and want to see him move forward and so it's a sort of criss-cross conversation all the time balancing this out, but it's hard to not become cynical. I genuinely think that he has come to Circles wanting to move forward and we just have to keep plugging away. The other core member was very much easier to fathom. He knew that he had this weakness and what caused the offences to take place. I think as long as he wasn't put in the same situation again, or if he was he would recognise what built up to the offences and take avoidance strategies and he'd cope. No, he was not as complex as the one we've got now.

As we sort of support him in moving out and doing various activities, and as he progresses, I think that helps you maintain the hope that he will build a life for himself beyond what he has at the moment. If he gets into paid employment and can actually make friendships – well, you can't see very far ahead, but each time he takes a step forward and does something positive you hope, well, maybe, maybe at the end of this…

The volunteers meet before the core member joins us. We talk about what we're going to do and then, afterwards, we discuss what has happened and we do have, not conflict exactly, but we all say what we feel about what has happened and our suspicions (if there are any), and we talk that through. Fortunately, we all get on extremely well and I don't think anybody goes away thinking, 'Oh, I wish they would keep quiet,' because it seems to work that way. I think it's quite a healthy sort of discussion afterwards.

[*There's an underlying unity there, is there?*] Oh absolutely, yes. I don't think we've ever gone away thinking it's been a disaster. There are good meetings and bad. This week we were quite high at the end of it because we felt he had actually progressed and we've actually tried something out: we tried reading aloud the minutes of the previous meeting at the beginning of the Circle meeting. This was because he's dyslexic. It was the best option to read it out loud and actually emphasise different things. It was after that he sparked off. I think we're evolving as a group and bring in new ideas as we go along. I think it would take you several years actually to get really effective. I hope we would continue together. Mind you, I suppose fresh life wouldn't hurt as long as you all gelled, but, yes, there are very forceful points put forward and we listen to each other.

What's most challenging is the intensity. At least one other person says they come away totally mentally exhausted at the end of it. That was true at the beginning and sometimes it's more exhausting than others.

[A core member has said to me that one of the good things about Circles is allowing you to talk about yourself.] Yes, I think that is the case. They've got someone who will listen, or several people who will listen, and won't criticise; just listen. I think that's the greatest thing you can give to anyone.

The first of our core members was interesting in the fact that he was so marked by being in prison. I remember saying to him, 'Can you walk down the street, go into shops?' And he said, 'No,' and I said, 'Do you feel as though you've got a mark on you?' and he said, 'Yes.' It was as bad as that, whereas the second one doesn't feel like that.

I think the first was marked by being a sex offender as well as being in prison. I haven't been in prison myself, but I had a long, long period in hospital – 17 weeks – and I remember going out into the street and being totally shocked by the number of people and the noise and the traffic. When I talk to them I think of the shock it must be of being out in what we call normality and they've been away for so much longer. It must be incredibly difficult coming back into that and not being free to tell people where they've come from, what they've done, possibly having no relatives or friends to support them. So to have somebody sit and listen to you would be incredible. The present core member hasn't said anything, but when we suggested that perhaps we should meet less frequently, it was like taking a chair away from underneath him. So the support must be there; they must need that support and value it.

When they were asking for volunteers [at the Quaker meeting], there were different reactions: both my husband and I are doing it, so we've talked to each other, but there was no one else interested in it – there was somebody actually that expressed some sort of revulsion at the thought, and I was surprised. I have friends who I know I can't mention it to because the interest they would show would be sort of voyeuristic and I don't think they would want to know how it worked as to what the ex-offender had done, and I just don't want that. I did come across somebody and I knew instantly she would be a perfect Circle member. The [regional] co-ordinator had been looking for somebody in her area and she's now been taken up and trained. I told her how we enjoy doing it and it's not a big commitment, but it is a regular commitment. She's open-minded, well balanced and she has a sense of humour. They're the Circles' qualities, I think. You need to be able to have a laugh and a curiosity about people because all offenders are just people, aren't they? You can't pick them out of a crowd.

Our children know we do it and they don't actually ask us about it. I think they're quite happy that we're doing it, but, yes, with small children, I also think it's too close to them.

Unless it's absolutely something that we've really got to thrash out between us, my husband doesn't let it come into the house with him. We talk on the way home sometimes. He'll talk about it for a short while and then I think he knows that I will go on sort of digging, trying to work things out, but he doesn't really want that. There have been occasions when we've examined something and then, I think, he feels that Circles shouldn't invade your life and mustn't take you over – which it could do if you worried about them [the core member]. It can go round and round in your head. And you do care about the core member.

It is tricky because we don't let on we're married. The dynamics [of the Circle] are very interesting in that respect because, occasionally, one of us has said something and it was quite obvious that we wouldn't know unless we lived together. So far the current core member hasn't picked up on it. He's very, very…not introverted, he's not exactly selfish, but he has very little empathy.

As to where you want to get the core member, I think it's to the point where they are feeling that they can cope on their own and live a reasonable life and that they know we're there to contact if they're really desperate. I think that it's necessary for them to know that they can do that because I know I would want to be able to do that. That would be the satisfactory conclusion really.

Geeta Patel: 'What I'm doing, I'm doing my part for the community'

Geeta Patel* is a lively, jocular, self-assured 24-year-old, whose first words to me are to excuse her appearance: she removes dark glasses to reveal a large plaster to cover an injury sustained when playing rugby. Her upbringing she describes as happy and sheltered, saying she was very protected by her parents, of whom she speaks affectionately. Her father is an Asian baker ('note the stereotype', she jokes), who was born in Mumbai, and her mother, who works in a supermarket, came to this country via Kenya. Geeta has an older brother, who attended a local university. She deliberately chose not to do so – something which is important to her in the kind of person she's become – and gained a degree in forensic psychobiology at the University of Abertay, Dundee. She is working as a receptionist in a sports injury clinic and with a beautician while she attempts to realise her ambition to be accepted at a university to take a master's in forensic psychology. She would like, in some way, to work with offenders. She had been a member of her Circle for four months at the time of the interview (September 2010). She says that she partly joined because of her interest in sex offenders; her wish to do something to help them manage their behaviour ('I am doing my bit for the community and that's important'); and also because she knows that such volunteering would stand her in good stead with universities considering her application for further study.

It all started when I went to Abertay University, Dundee. It was basically a psychology-based degree with a lot of forensics put in. We had two specific forensic psychology modules that looked at sex offenders, and we started to learn about where a criminal kind of behaviour can originate from, such as brain damage. A lot of what we looked at could be stuff like interaction with their parents when they were growing up, the kind of role models they had. The more I learnt, the more I started to feel that there's a side of these people which the media never portrays and I kind of wanted to know more about it. It's so easy for the average Joe just to think, you know, 'What I read in the paper is exactly how it is,' when, in reality, the more you look into the mechanics of the criminal mind you actually realise these people, whether they're sex offenders or just criminals, are not just what they seem to be on the surface.

---

* Geeta Patel is a pseudonym.

How I came to know about Circles is actually quite a funny story. When I'd finished university, that summer I applied for my masters in forensic psychology and I didn't get through. I got through to interview stage and they said, 'There's people above you who've had more experience and that's how it goes.' You know, it's very competitive and I fully understand and I've come back to my boss [at the sports injury clinic] and said, 'Obviously, it was a little bit of a knock because, you know, I always assumed I'd go from one degree to a master's straight to where I wanted to go, and in reality it's not happened like that.' So she goes, 'Right, OK, let's think of the positive – what did they say?' When I didn't get in, I asked the person who interviewed me at the university what to do and they said, 'Just work hard, get as much experience as you can working with offenders, with alcoholics, anything which could lead to any kind of criminal behaviour, anything like that.' So my boss and me were looking on-line – I'm very lucky she was also helping me out as much as she could – and a couple of police guys would come in here and she would always mention to them if there's projects they know of that I might take part in.

So she knew that I was looking for volunteering within the offender field and it turns out that someone who was a Circle project manager actually came along to the clinic and, obviously, my boss talks to them about what they do and one thing led to another and I had an email – 'cause I was actually on holiday at the time – waiting for me when I came back with this Circles' project manager's number asking me to ring them to get involved in the project if I wanted to. So it was just total fate, without question; total, total luck.

My initial thoughts [about the Circle] were that for the first time I'm actually going to interact one-on-one with an offender. Obviously, we're in a group of four but at the end of the day I can think of it as being me and them because it's how I feel about it, and I was thinking I don't know how they were going to take me, how I was going to take them, but I thought, you know, if I go in there with a positive frame of mind, I can take how I want to whatever's said, and so, yeah, it went from there.

In my training we had an array of people from different walks of life and the group I was working with were all kinds of professions – for example, we had a probation officer, an ex-police officer. When we're doing this role play they seemed to take more charge because obviously they had more experience with this field and I kind of found myself thinking, a) I could learn from them, but b) thinking maybe this wasn't for me, but, then, at the end of the day, they're years older than me, they've had the experience which I've not had, and this is the ideal opportunity for me to kind of get, in five, six years, where they are, so, it was just ideal.

I just wanted to go along and maybe do something for this offender which people don't seem to do, which is actually listen to them. We found, with our core member, that no one's given him the chance in life: he wants to get a job, he wants to get a new property, he wants to move on in his life, but, unfortunately, the fact that he's got a criminal record straight away means that no one's going to give him a chance. Obviously, it's totally justified in a way, but, then, on the other hand, with these people who he's applying to, where do their perceptions of criminals come from? Again, this is the whole kind of concept where the media over-exaggerates everything and you think, 'If these people really knew...'

I've been very lucky in my circle. Our core member is quite responsive, he actually feels he wants to change, but I've also been talking to people who I've trained with [for Circles] and they've not had the same experiences that we've had with our core member. I mean, their core member actually decided to reoffend, break his licence, and I look at our core member now and think if I'd had their core member I don't think I would have had the reinforcement as I have had with our core member.

Our Circle is quite interesting. We four volunteers get on very well. There's two mature ladies and there's two younger ones – the other one is 26; I don't know how old the others are, just mature. We're an all-female group. One member has spent the latter part of her life working with offenders – she volunteers at prisons and so on. Another is actually at university studying (I think) criminology and psychology and the third is studying something along the same lines, so we've all kind of had the same background in that way, but we've got different levels of understanding and we've got different tolerances.

We always wanted to make it as relaxed as possible; we didn't want it to feel like we're interrogating our core member so our meeting time turned out to be at 12.30 pm so we then came up with the idea that everyone brings lunch, and you sit and eat and just chat. That way it kind of helps him [the core member] to calm down. This has meant that we didn't have to feel like it was regimented – 'Right, so, OK, today we're going to ask five questions. Right: one, two, three, four, five.' Initially you may think that's going to happen but never ever can you plan for a meeting.

There's been times when we've said, 'Last meeting we talked about fantasies and this week we will talk more about this,' then we'll go to the next meeting and it turns out he's had two job rejections and he's really down. You can't kind of go to the fantasy bit because you have to deal with his mental state because the idea is if he's so low, as a group, you want to pick him up, to motivate him to move on. Our role is to help him become a member of society, and help him focus on himself.

But the mechanics of the group are great. We all say what we need to do, we've got a member who's maybe slightly more worldly so she's a lot more kind of dubious about what our core member says, and she's great for the group. The core member leaves the meeting room and then we spend the last half an hour of the time just going over anything we want to air so we don't take it home. And the worldly one'll say stuff like, oh, say, 'Did you think about what was actually behind him saying this or that?' and the rest of us'll think, 'Do you know, that's really something which we didn't even think about at the time.' But it's great to have someone like that in your group because it means everyone learns from it and everyone gets to contribute what we can. So, I say, our core member's very lucky [*laughs*].

Don't get me wrong: it's taken a long time to get to where we are with our relationship as four volunteers working together. We've always been of the understanding that we're the foundation which our core member's going to thrive on, and we spent a lot of time initially breaking ground with each other. We have a Circles phone so the core member can interact with us. Each week, if anything's wrong, he can text or ring. We keep nothing from each other and we made sure the core member knew that we didn't hide anything from each other, so, for example, if he'd rung me I'd say to him: 'You do realise, you know, that whatever we've said today I will email the rest of the group?' and at the next meeting I will reinforce that. In that way he knew that he could never take advantage of just one of us. I think that kind of belief helped our relationship grow, because, at the end of the day, we were four strangers who all come to Circles for our own reasons.

[*Did you find it curious that you should sit and discuss quite intimate details – his sex life, his fantasies, what he's done – with this man?*] That has never really bothered me because I think this is the reinforced part. I know that if I was ever traumatised by anything I could lean on my other volunteers. We have been a great support for each other. Initially, we didn't break ground with the core member by asking, 'What's your sex life like?', we worked on building a rapport with him. We would say we grew up doing this and ask what he grew up doing. And, then, he voluntarily brought along a life timeline [which shows the long-term context in which to examine the offender's antecedents – for example, offending behaviour, looking for clues as to why he acted as he did]. That's when he started opening up about his first sexual experience, his sexual experiences and his growing up. We learnt a lot just from that and we didn't have to instigate him telling us about it. It was a good sign 'cause it's him showing that he trusted us, so it gave us a confidence to start saying to him, oh, I don't know, but, say, 'So, when you see a little girl or a little boy on the street, what kind of feelings do you get, what do you think about?' It's that initial opening up to us which gave us a kind of green light to start delving deeper, but we kind of eased ourselves into it. Nothing shocked us, 'cause we kind of, like, expected at some point we were going to hear about the ins and outs of his offence.

[*Do you feel a sort of responsibility for the trust that he's giving you?*] Oh, yes, of course I do, because he's opening up to things which he's never been able to speak to people about, because as soon as he's spoken to someone about it he's mostly been shunned or the door's just been slammed in his face. It's a big transition for us to be able to talk to him, but it's the bigger transition, I think, really for our core member because…well, if you're an alcoholic, for example, you can go to an Alcoholics Anonymous group and you can openly say to people, 'I'm Joe Bloggs and I'm addicted to alcohol.' Where can he go? Who can he talk to about his addiction – because you can argue that it is an addiction – and all of a sudden he's got four people in front of him who a) are wanting to listen to him; b) aren't willing to judge him; and c), most importantly, aren't going to go away.

I remember our first meeting with our core member when we learnt about his offence and the first thing he said to us was, 'Now that you know about my offence I won't be offended if none of you want to carry on in the Circle.' That kind of took me aback because I was kind of, like, what he's saying here is what he's experienced, what he's expected of people; he's always had to deal with people just walking away from his life. There was someone who was meant to be his closest friend whom he thought he could share everything with and it's tough, yeah.

One side of me is thinking that is absolutely horrendous: how can you imagine doing that? But then the kind of academic side of me's saying, 'You've got to think why, why has he done what he's done, what's led him to do it?' I've got a core member in front of me who genuinely seems like he regrets what he did. I can argue to a certain extent that he still thinks it's smaller than what he actually did in reality; he doesn't realise how big an offence it was but he's having to reap the consequences now, for example by not getting jobs, being turned away. I'm not very judgemental, I try and understand them and not make assumptions, but, obviously, I don't condone the crime at all. Now the group which I was talking about – where their core member reoffended – it turns out that he had offended at a much higher level than our offender. Had that been our offender it may have made it very, very different, but my first experience initially, in reality, was that what he did wasn't as bad as it could have been.

However, now I'm getting to know him more, I'm starting to be a lot more dubious about what he's saying to me. For example, he's apparently spending three hours every day looking online at jobs, yet finding nothing which he would want to apply for. On the other hand, he'll come back to me and he'll say, 'I had a really good week, a really productive week, I did that, I did a), b) and c),' and you think, 'Hang on, last week you had that kind of week and all of a sudden you're just telling me this and this.' He's learnt from our reaction from the week before, and thinks, 'Right, I'm gonna start telling them what they want to hear, so if they ask me if I went shopping and did I see any children, I'm gonna say, "Yes I did but I used my distraction method, which I learnt on my [sex offender treatment] programme and it was fine. I looked at my phone or I just went home because I didn't want to be in that situation."' That's perfect, our core member's a diamond, a total gem, and he's great and this programme has totally converted him into this saint, but you know, in spite of what I said and meant very positively about him earlier, you think…mmm, you know…

I think in our group I was the last one to question what he's saying, just because I've had no interaction with offenders before and I always thought he was going to be great, he's going to listen to us. Initially, he was great, he was listening to us, taking on board everything we were saying and then all of a sudden things started happening. One week we were chatting afterwards and people were saying, oh he said this, but then last week he said this, he said five-year-old last week and this week he said eight-year-old, and then people start cross-referencing. That's why the group works so well, because it's things like that which we could pick up on. More importantly, when someone starts to make these cross-references, our project manager will make us realise we need to help integrate our core member into society and not over-analyse everything he says. Look at the bigger picture, not the little picture.

I think [a healthy scepticism] is something which everyone who's going to work with offenders needs to have, and I think this Circle has given me the opportunity to actually learn to grow that part of my personality. I think it's important because, you know, I'm not saying that every time he's saying something I'm thinking, 'Oh my God, no you didn't,' that I'm thinking the total worst, that I am always doubting him.

I've been very lucky that the people I've always had around me are people I've never had to be sceptical about; I've always had the kind of conventional '2.4 children' kind of life, where I've had the two parents, the brother. I've always had a good home life, everything, so I've never had the need to doubt anything in my life 'cause of everything around me.

[The big challenge of the Circle] has been learning to get to know my fellow volunteers, because you have that meeting each week where you don't want to step on anyone's toes, you don't want to interrupt anyone if someone's saying something which you think you know, or which makes no sense, or doesn't need to be said, or doesn't need to be expanded on. It's taken me a long time to be able to say, 'Do you know what, I don't think we need to talk about that…I think we need to step back to this… We need to talk about this or let's go back to that in a minute.' It took a long time before I could actually say to the rest of my group at the end of the meeting, 'You know what, you annoyed me a little bit – I don't think you had to press him about that. I don't think it was really fair.' We've always been of the attitude that if we have an issue with each other we never, never express it in front of our core member. As far as he's concerned we're four very tight-knit people who he cannot break. That's the biggest challenge, but, then again, all through life you have to learn to make friends, learn to tolerate other people and this is just another example. But, in this case, you see these people once a week for two and a half hours and for one and a half hours of that you've got a fifth person there, so in the half an hour before and the half an hour after, that's all you have to really get to know these people.

I'm not saying I know everything about human beings but I've not learnt anything I didn't know already. I know people can tell the truth, I know people can lie, I know people react differently to totally different situations. For example, our core member likes to play computer games, and he came to one meeting and he said he'd not played the games all week. To me that was a big thing – this is his life and he's not done it for a whole week. Afterwards, I said to my fellow volunteers, 'Does this not worry you?' And them saying it's just one week, it's not the end of the world, and I could see that they're right. So, maybe, in some respects, it's maybe stopped me being over-analytical about what's being said to me. So, just take a step back and just let things go, settle down. As it is, the following week he was fine – he'd played his games. An example of differing interpretations of the same information.

The past few weeks for me have been really cognitively demanding, it's been like pounding a brick wall with him. We'll say to him, 'You should go shopping.' 'I'm not going shopping. Why should I go shopping?' he'll say. 'I can do whatever I like, I don't need to do that, I can stay in my house, I don't need to leave it.' It's just been like that and then the next moment he'd say, 'Oh, I need to go shopping,' and so you're going round in a circle and we're all drained, we're all looking at our clocks – and we've never had to do it before – to see when the time's going to run out. He turned around and said at the end of one of the meetings, 'I know I'm being very difficult at the moment. I'm very low, but I hope you guys realise I really do appreciate what you are doing for me.' And you've got to understand that it is an actual perk because how many people in life actually get to go meet a group of people and tell them what they've done in the week – you don't. Some people around don't even get to tell their partners what they're planning in a week. This core member's coming to us, can tell us anything about his week, whether it be something as simple as he went for a job or something as deep as he found himself going to the park because there were kids there.

My family know that I work with an offender. I've chosen not to disclose to them what type of offender I work with, mainly because I've led a very sheltered life (which is why university was so important for me). I have a very protective family, who don't want me exposed to anything that is going to harm me. My very close friends have always known about my motivation to work with criminals, my lack of fear to work with sex offenders, with the most extreme kind of criminals if I had the chance to. So, with my very close friends, as soon as I told them I'd be working with this project called Circles, and with sex offenders, their first reaction was, 'That's great, that's going to help you get on to your master's,' 'cause they all know that my motivation is to get on to this master's course and this is a way – as well as other reasons – of helping to do that.

Yes, I could go and work with young offenders or other kinds of offender, lower-risk offenders, but what I'd say to that [if someone asked me why I did not do that] is, 'What you know about sex offenders is what you know from the media. Do you actually know that in reality there could be about 20 people walking around you who are sex offenders? We can't lock them up forever, they're going to be out in society, and people who do Circles or people who work one-on-one with offenders like sex offenders, the kind of surveillance they provide is so important to the community. Obviously, these people are motivated to commit offences again, they obviously have sexual urges, they're human after all, and, I think, if it wasn't for people like me these people would just be walking around and get to do what they want, because in reality we can't afford to keep thousands of sex offenders in prison, it's just not feasible.'

Quite a few of my fellow degree people are really interested in what I've been doing and without question I would recommend them [to volunteer for a Circle]. A lot of them have asked how I am dealing with it psychologically; how I feel about it; am I being looked after? And do you know what, it's not had any kind of the impact on my personal life or on my emotional well-being that I thought maybe could have happened, when I learnt about my offender's offence. But then that's reinforced by the fact I don't think my offender's offence is as bad as others.

None of my friends, who are just average – I mean they haven't been to university but have gone off and done hairdressing or worked as beauticians, et cetera – have ever wanted to be part of the project, but the people I've been on a degree with – across the country – they've shown interest. This shows how one person can spread the word about a project when I didn't know of it until, as I said, this person happened to walk into my place of work and one thing led to another. It's just fate.

One of my friends was actually looking into the Circles project in her area, but she said that what put her off is the fact that she's not able to commit to 12 months [the minimum time for a Circle]. We're all graduates and we're all looking for jobs, whereas to me 12 months – I thought, right, that's fine. Time has already flown by and I cannot believe we are already four months into our time together. I know for a fact if I was to say to my co-ordinator [of the regional Circles project], 'I can't deal with this any more,' I know that there are ways where she can de-select me, because at the end of the day it's my well-being that they're going to be concerned about.

[*Do you think this has anything to do with your emotional resilience and what sounds like a strong attachment to your parents?*] Yes, I think it really has. My parents have always...I'm very lucky I've had...obviously my mum and dad are still together which is not heard of for lots of people.

They've always told me things like don't walk on the underpass, and this, that and the other. When I've gone home my mum's always asked me how my day's been, and I've been able to tell her, so I've always been able to open up about things. I think that I've always been a strong person, because, you know, I always wanted to protect my parents from anything which was upsetting me because I didn't want to worry them. So I've learnt to lean on other people and I've learnt to build up this kind of resilience, as you said, and just been able to cope with what's going on in life. I've got a great, great attitude towards life: I try look at the funny/positive things in life, I try to just be happy as much as I can. I think doing this I always look at the positive. What I'm doing, I'm doing for my part for the community and I think that's important.

I've also been helping out with the [Circles] trainees [volunteers] and when you see people coming along it just reminds you they're all kind of sitting there, kind of not knowing what to say to each other, and I think, 'Four months ago, five months ago, that was me' and look at me now. Maybe I envy them starting off now because I would like to be at the beginning and for that to last that little bit longer. I talk to the people I trained with, I look forward to seeing them. We're having a Christmas do, so I'm looking forward to finding out how they're getting on. We all have our different motivations for doing this, but it's just a great, great experience.

Maybe it's given me the drive, that little bit more to pursue my future of working with offenders and furthering my psychology aspirations. I don't think it's changed me as a person, but maybe I've opened up a little bit, thinking there are more people out there who actually have committed crimes.

If I have become a little less analytical maybe that's because I know that I don't need to be because my fellow volunteers have kind of almost spread out responsibility for that. Deep down, I don't know why subconsciously I'm doing this, but it may well be because I feel very, very safe knowing that I if I miss something the others are going to pick up on it. I've never had to worry about that, and if I was to think something was a small matter (or a big matter) I know that the rest of my group would respond in a way which would make me feel happy. But, again, it's taken a long time to get to that stage. It's not easy, but I think we're there as a group. Definitely in a great place with each other and our core member.

My time in the Circle has been really positive and if circumstances allow it, then I can already foresee myself in a second Circle in nine months' time.

Seona Angell: 'I think maybe people think I am a bit quirky for doing it'

The large house is in a pleasant village, 40 minutes from the nearest railway station. A stone bridge across a stream cuts the large garden from the field at the back where, not so long ago, Seona Angell kept horses. This seems a long way away from her and three colleague volunteers sitting in a small room meeting with their core member. But these are worlds within which she seemingly unselfconsciously moves. She joined her Circle in August 2009 but before that she had been appointed assistant co-ordinator for her local Circles project, a job she had only recently regrettably given up, due to lack of funding, when we met (November 2010). But this was far from being her introduction to the world of offending. For some years she has worked with young offenders as a member of a youth offending team lay panel and she also works with NSPCC professionals on assessing those suspected of child abuse and their partners. What she describes as her secure and privileged life began as a PA, where, among others, she worked for both the fashion designer Mary Quant and her husband Alexander Plunkett-Green, and the keeper of the mineralogy at the (then) British Museum (Natural History), which is now known as the Natural History Museum. Two children – now adults – interrupted her working life, although during that period she took various courses including two on counselling ('I never knew when it might come in handy'). Today, when not engaged in her time-consuming voluntary roles, she works with her husband in his busy financial advisory business.

Eight and a half years ago I started doing referral panel work with the local youth offending team which involves meeting young people who've gone to court for the first time, and have then been convicted and charged with an offence and given a referral order. They come to a panel meeting, which comprises two fully trained community panel members and a youth justice officer, where a contract is formed and they have to work to complete this contract successfully in order to have a spent conviction.

Some of these offences are quite serious and a few include young people who have sexually harmed and have been charged for sexual offending behaviours. Through this voluntary work I got to know some of the NSPCC professionals who were working with those young people. After several years of contact with the NSPCC I was approached by the

NSPCC manager and asked if I would be prepared to undertake some voluntary work with adult sex offenders. I said I was interested and keen to do that.

That process took a long time to come to fruition, and, while I was waiting, the NSPCC manager asked if I had heard of Circles, and would I like to work with them. Well, I hadn't heard of Circles, I didn't know what Circles were, so he gave me a brief overview and I said, yes, I liked the idea and was keen to learn more. Coming from a restorative justice background with the youth offending team where one's role is to support young people and hold them accountable for their offending behaviour, I felt that this was something that was parallel in a way – different, but parallel – and something that I could relate to, believe in and contribute towards. With young people, I strongly believe that they aren't born bad and I actually feel the same about sex offenders: when they were born they weren't born sex offenders.

Thus, I felt I had something I could offer Circles and felt it was something I would like to do and could do. It was strange in a way because initially I was asked if I would be prepared to support the new Circles co-ordinator as an assistant. I said I would be happy to do this and so undertook the co-ordinator training at Circles UK in Reading. Subsequently I said, 'Well, that's great, but actually I'd like to be part of a Circle, I'd like to be a volunteer, I'd like to know what they're about and experience being a volunteer on a Circle.' Thus, I undertook the volunteer training and became a Circles volunteer, doing so in a sort of backwards way because my volunteer training happened after my co-ordinator training. In August 2009, I was placed on my first Circle (the first in my county).

[*Would you say your attitude has changed at all as a result of this experience?*] No, that remains: I'm quite adamant that people aren't born bad; that perhaps society and what happens to people makes them bad. The sex offenders that I encounter through my Circles work have done horrendous things but aren't necessarily horrendous people. I would stand by that, so my attitude in that respect hasn't changed, but my eyes have been opened, more so, I think, with the adults than with the young people I've worked with.

Saying my eyes have been opened reflects just what people have been through out there – a lot of the sex offenders I've met and worked with (not all but some of them) have been abused as children and whilst that in no way condones their behaviours, it gives me some insight into perhaps what's gone wrong and why. I suppose if I'm honest, I've had a very privileged life in that I've been brought up in a happy and loving family, without ever having experienced any kind of abuse. Therefore, my eyes have been opened because sometimes I just can't believe what I am hearing, and that's sometimes been quite hard, but it has been, and will continue to be, a learning curve. I think that it's this which keeps me going with Circles work – I want to learn more and, in a way, I want to try and help so that children in the future don't have to go through those awful things, and some of what I've heard has been really awful and quite disturbing.

I've now nearly completed one full Circle [the Circle was due to end in February 2011] and I know we have made a difference. We've been working with a very isolated character, an older man, a very aggressive, angry man who is now much less aggressive, much less angry and who over the past 15, 16 months hasn't reoffended and I believe he would have done so had he not had the Circle. So, yes, I think we've made a big difference.

At the moment we're down to meeting every six to eight weeks with phone contact in between. He's never been a great one for picking up the phone although he knows he can if he wants to, but I do worry [about when the Circle ends] because of his isolation and although he says he isn't lonely and likes being on his own, I believe he is lonely and that is a concern for me. I think because of that I would probably – and so would my three Circle colleagues – make sure we ring once a month, maybe less than that as time goes on, but we will keep in touch with him because I think we all do feel that there will be a gap and a void in his life when the Circle ends. He says he doesn't want a Circle, he's often indicated he'd like it to end, but actually I think he'll miss it when it's not there.

[*Given your experience of Circles as an assistant co-ordinator, are Circles determined by who the core member is?*] Yes, I would say definitely. I mean, our core member is unique in that he…well, he's a very difficult character and he's a character who sparks off at the slightest thing. Although he's agreed to have a Circle he is basically in denial, which has made it quite difficult and challenging for us as Circle volunteers. With the other Circles I've sat in on, the core members are much more – dare I say? – compliant, approachable and who may, on the surface, appear to want help more than our core member does, and perhaps want to turn their lives around more and not to reoffend. So I would say, yes, he is very different, whilst with other Circles I've been to, you've got the typical core member who will say, 'Well, yes, I really do want help and

I will come to Circle meetings and say to you I've had these thoughts, I've had these feelings – I saw a little girl or boy walking along the street and I shouldn't be feeling like that. Help me – what can I do about that?' We've never experienced that with our core member, because he's basically been in denial about his offences or certainly about there being anything wrong with his offences, saying they were just loving relationships.

I knew one of the volunteers well through my work at the youth offending team; in fact, I introduced him to Circles. With one of the others, I knew her husband very well and her quite well. The other one I didn't know at all prior to our training. The two volunteer colleagues I knew through my field of working with young people who'd offended (not necessarily offended sexually) had experience, but the fourth whom I didn't know had no experience at all. That was really interesting, and because of having no previous experience he had a different perspective which proved to be a really good balancing factor. He claims that he's learnt huge amounts from us; however, I would say we've equally learnt from him – it has worked extremely well.

We helped him [the fourth volunteer] with his understanding of perhaps where this core member was coming from and not necessarily to take everything at face value. He's taken that on board very quickly and demonstrated a very open approach which was very beneficial for us as well. He would come in without a background of any experience of working with people who'd offended and say, 'Well, hey, what about this?' and 'Am I right in thinking that?' On one-to-one talking with our core member, this volunteer has been excellent and, ironically enough, has similar interests to our core member, so this has been quite a positive conversation point in our meetings. On balance, it's worked exceptionally well with two women, two men; two are retired, and I work pretty well full-time doing all sorts of things, and the other volunteer works part-time, so we're all different.

The most challenging thing has been the presenting behaviour of our core member. He can be extremely volatile and angry, and whilst this isn't necessarily directed at the volunteers, it's usually directed against the police, whom he hates with a vengeance: he calls them the Gestapo and at times says he believes we are spies for the Gestapo. There have been occasions at meetings when he has become physically very angry with himself – not towards us – almost to the point of him shaking, raising his voice, using foul language and talking over others. This is one area where I feel we've been very successful, because our core member had very few social skills and we've actually taught him that it's not helpful when you're with a group of people to shout over them, to not allow them to answer your questions and not to listen. We've always listened to him and we've tried to train him over the last 16 months to actually pause and listen for the response before bowling in and shouting or screaming across people – and, believe you me, 'screaming' is not an exaggeration. So I guess that's really been the most challenging thing. His behaviours have actually been quite exhausting; for example, a meeting that lasts for two hours with constant shouting.

[*How do you keep under control what I will call perhaps your natural instinct to leave when there's your Circles instinct is to be there for him?*] Well, there have been two or three occasions when he's become so exasperated, feeling that perhaps we are there as spies, as he calls it, where he's said, 'That's it, you're not my friends, you're just here to spy and I'm off' (but he never actually went). There have also been times when his behaviour has been such that we may all have thought, 'I don't know how much more we can take of this,' but that would have only been momentary and, on reflection, we would actually have been quite sad if he hadn't come back. On one occasion he left in a fairly angry mood, but we've never quite lost him, and we have always said to him, 'We'll be here next week and we hope you come,' and he has always turned up. However, I think there have been moments when we might have been (if I'm honest) almost relieved in a way if he had got up and walked out. That's obviously on a personal level, but clearly we are all aware that our role is to accept that his anger isn't directed at us, hard though that has been at times.

I think if I hadn't had the experience of working with difficult young people over many years, in meetings where obviously with young people you're very much the adult and the older person (and this is perhaps different because, in fact, he's older than us), our experiences would have been more difficult. This is where the four of us have been really good for each other. Possibly, the Circle member without the former experience might have found it more difficult to sit through such tirades, but one of the members of our Circle is a fairly senior retired social worker who's well used to that kind of presenting behaviour and this has been helpful. So, yes, there have been times when we've just wanted to chuck in the towel but in reality we would never have done so. I think what's made it easier is past experience and I don't know that any training could prepare you for the things that we've had thrown at us – luckily we support each other and there's a wealth of experience within our Circle that's enabled us to ride the storm – and at times it has been quite a storm.

What's been really rewarding is that there are many occasions when we feel we've made two steps forward, albeit sometimes a couple back as well. There are many occasions at the end of meetings where we've been really quite encouraged by him perhaps not shouting as much, or him not disagreeing with us as much, or even possibly listening to us more, and, of course, the most encouraging factor being that he hasn't reoffended. Yes, we have been hugely uplifted by that, and I have to say we do like him – he is a very likeable character.

I feel if we save one child, even one, in the future from being the victim of abuse, then it's got to be worth it. I've talked to my husband, who is wonderful about this, a lot about the ethos behind Circles, the ethos behind the 'No more victims', and the purpose of it and what we're trying to achieve and the goals and so forth. He's a great support and I do talk to him – always anonymously. Sometimes, if we've had a really bad meeting I'll say, 'Oh, gosh that was awful.' He listens and is a great sounding board.

I think if I'd started to do this before having done the youth offending team work that I've been doing with the young people for so long, he might have questioned whether Circles was a good idea and he once said to me, 'Hang on a minute, you're not going to be meeting on your own with possibly violent or aggressive sex offenders, are you?' I reassured him saying, 'No, that's not how it works.' So, yes, that question of doubt and concern for my well-being was there but he has faith in my judgement and is very sensible, pragmatic and utterly supportive. My children are 29 and 27 now and are also very supportive, encouraging and complimentary about what they see as a job that not many other people would want to do.

As for friends, I think people are very interested, but as a starting point I don't really talk to many people about my work other than close family or friends. If people ask me what I do I say, 'I do some voluntary work around child protection,' and leave it at that, or 'I do something for the NSPCC and there's an organisation called Circles that works with offenders in the community,' but I don't go into specifics and that usually satisfies their curiosity.

However, there are people who know me better and do know what I do, listen to what I have to say and find it very interesting. The usual comment is, 'Well, I would never do that, I couldn't do that, I don't know how you do that, I think you're mad to do that, is it safe for you to do that?' But we're very risk-aware and supervised and supported, and work closely with police and probation.

I think once most people know what I do, they then don't really want to talk about it and just refer to 'the work that you do'; it's 'it' [*she laughs*]. People feel uncomfortable with the subject. So it's funny – I don't give them details but even the very basics become 'it'. 'It' is kind of removed and, I think, people think and want 'it' to be a world apart – it's outside our world, it happens out there, it's in the street, it's in the town, everybody knows it happens but it doesn't affect us. That's when I actually inform people, 'Well, actually, yes, it does, it does hugely, and these sex offenders are not all just your down-and-outs and your people who are not educated and can't read and write. It can be quite the opposite.' Then I'll often talk to them about these Catholic priests, and say, 'Come on, isn't it good that at last someone is finding out that these things happened and how appalling it is (it should never have happened) so that hopefully it won't happen in the future?' They can kind of relate to that – at a distance.

No, not one of them, absolutely not one of them [has ever thought they might want to volunteer], and I've never asked them because I know they wouldn't. I think they just think I'm a bit quirky. As I often say to them, 'Well, we're all different and we all do things for various reasons and, thank goodness, we all do different things. You're right, somebody has got to do it, but it's not just that I have to do it; I actually enjoy what I do and I don't mind saying I enjoy it because I don't think I would do it if I didn't enjoy it. I find it rewarding, I find it challenging and I feel I've something I am able to give to it.'

[*When you were only working with young people, were friends more sympathetic?*] Oh yes, because the work with the young people involves a criminal justice process, so that's kind of 'acceptable'. A lot of questions would be asked about that and I would respond, anonymising the young people, saying, 'Gosh, these young people who get into trouble and offend, you know there's always a history, they don't generally come from loving, caring homes. I've met hundreds of young people, and I've yet to find one on a referral order that's come from a truly loving, caring and supportive home. I believe that across the board and across the classes, the one thing that stops young people getting into trouble is a loving and caring family. This basically is why I do it.' It's interesting because this can be a talking point and they can relate to that, but you can then say, 'Young people, too, commit quite serious offences such as sexual offences,' and you may then get the response, 'Oh, really, well how strange...', but when the conversation shifts to adult sex offenders, it's a kind of a closed door and I find this hostile.

I think probably some of them would consider young people as yobs in the town and such stereotypes, but with adults I think much of the resentment is to do with media coverage of sex offenders which can be very detrimental and judgemental. People pick up on that, you know, the seedy adult in the overcoat, et cetera. I suppose perhaps when it's children, they'll be a little bit more sympathetic or a little bit more understanding, often saying, 'Oh, that must be the parents' fault.' They are happy to detract the blame in this way but once you're an adult, well, that's different. I don't push what I do that much so I probably don't get into really in-depth conversations. I did once, when I was invited to some friends for supper whom I know very well. There was one other couple there whom I didn't know and he was particularly pompous and arrogant and very detrimental towards young people, calling them yobs in the street, et cetera. I said very little but my friend, who vaguely knew the kind of work I was doing, raised the issue and I almost got a verbal assault from this guy about being some pussy-footing do-gooder, so much so that when pudding had finished he got up, left and walked out!

That was relating to young people but there was also an occasion when someone I know invited me to play tennis at her friend's house. We were having coffee in her kitchen after the game and her husband, whom I had never met, was there and he asked me what I did. I said something like voluntary 'child protection work', but he kept digging – you know, 'Yes?', 'And?' – until I just said, 'I work with adult sex offenders in the community' – the walls went up and the shutters came down immediately. He left the room, didn't say goodbye and I have never seen him since.

If one of my friends was interested, I suppose I'd ask, 'If you want to do voluntary work, what are you expecting to get out of it?' Then I would wait to see what they said. I think I would tell them about Circles more from a factual viewpoint: how it works, the training, what's expected of you, the time involvement, that you'll get your petrol paid, one meeting a week or maybe a fortnight. I'd talk about confidentiality being obviously a huge part of the work. I'd say that they needed to get in touch with a co-ordinator and give them some idea of what they would be expected to do and then I might put on my volunteer's hat and say from my perspective how very rewarding it is – I might say that although we've had a very difficult core member, I've still got a huge amount out of it.

I've put people in touch with the youth offending teams in their area but I've never done so with Circles or the NSPCC. When I tell people I work for the NSPCC they immediately think (it is quite extraordinary how they have this stereotype image) of me with a pair of earphones on and a telephone in my hand on ChildLine, because that's what NSPCC volunteers do. In some ways, what I do for Circles is the same kind of work as with the NSPCC. People are generally very pleased somebody does it, but they couldn't see themselves doing it and they think perhaps I'm a bit odd for doing it. That's how I think I'm perceived.

From a personal point of view, I've met some really nice people [through Circles]. I've learnt a lot, and am constantly learning on the job as well as from ongoing training that we are given. It's a continual learning process. If things go well at a meeting, however small it is, I get a real buzz and kick out of that; it makes you feel lighter of step so that whilst driving home you think, 'I've achieved something today, that's really good.' It gives you a lift, it makes you feel better and it makes you feel as if you're doing something not just for yourself – 'cause I always feel that you get more, much more of a kick out of giving than taking. Then there are those meetings when it's not so good and you may think, 'Gosh, why am I doing this?' But I know why I'm doing it: this kind of work for the wrong reason is not only very unhelpful for yourself, but it's also very unhelpful for the core members.

[*Did you ever have to think through those issues yourself?*] No, I didn't really. I mean, it's fairly typical of me that if I decide I want to do something and I believe in it, then I will do it. I am quite a strong-willed person and I will always do anything I take on to the best of my ability. I'll give it 110 per cent; I may not get that back but I'll give it my all. I believe so passionately in this kind of work and I believe that if someone has committed these horrendous offences – and they really are awful – and they've, for example, been to prison and served their time and perhaps done a [sex offender treatment] programme, come out and said that they want to try to reintegrate, to rehabilitate and not to offend again, then we are doing them a disservice if we don't help them to do just that. It's no good just isolating them as if they're a leper in the community because all they'll do is offend again. That sounds very clichéd but it is really true. I suppose that's what drives me and, therefore, I've never really questioned it.

Chapter 6

But Does It Work?

EVALUATION AND EVIDENCE

Stephen Hanvey

There is a highly attractive conceptual simplicity behind the Circles model. Trained local volunteers, in touch with statutory agencies, counteract the loneliness and isolation so likely to contribute to sexual reoffending. The concept is not rocket science as interventions go, but the increasing acceptance of, and support for the model by statutory agencies indicates an appreciation that Circles are, indeed, effective. The review of the Criminal Justice Joint Inspection of HMI Probation and HMI Constabulary (2010) into the management of sex offenders in the community notes the highly beneficial contribution of Circles in one of the localities inspected where they were operating. It notes that 'community reintegration was given adequate attention by most probation trusts and some good practice examples were found, including the use of COSA [Circles of Support and Accountability] and schemes to support offenders in independent accommodation' (p.47).

The conclusion was that 'the importance of this work in preventing further reoffending needed to be better recognised' (paras 8.17 and 8.18). But just how the impact and effectiveness of Circles can be objectively and credibly evaluated and presented is a vexed question. This is not, those involved in Circles would argue, because of inherent frailties or flaws in the model, but rather due to the challenge of finding an accepted path across the shifting sands of criminological research, particularly at a time of unprecedented political and financial pressures.

Therefore, this chapter will attempt to explore the means by which this service is seeking to prove itself worthy of its claims to be making a highly effective community-based impact in reducing sexual reoffending. If efficacy can be accepted, then the sequitur as to cost-effectiveness, it is suggested, is provided as well. No comparison between a community-based voluntary programme providing effective support and additional monitoring and the alternative of prolonged criminal proceedings, costly custodial sentences and the human suffering of multiple offences is going to be other than a resounding affirmation for Circles as resources well spent.

Before presenting the various means by which Circles have been arguing their case using data which can be objectively analysed and interpreted, it is worth examining the context for the development of such a model and the consequences for its further progression and direction, in the light of key criminal justice and rehabilitation concepts. This is not to be an academic review of the research findings on Circles to date, although some are included below, but rather a broader exploration as to how the evidence has been assembled and the influences to which that process is subject. (Indeed, the reader will be mindful that a bias towards evidence supporting the development of Circles may be somewhat inevitable in a book of this nature.) No systematic review of all the research was undertaken, but reference is made to the key studies, still admittedly limited in number given the relative newness of the model.

A retributive justice–restorative justice continuum

A particular question for those assessing the success of Circles has often been to ask which lens should be used to view its work and achievements. With one foot firmly in the world of retributive criminal justice targets and the other in community-based programmes drawing on restorative justice principles a certain tension may be felt. This tension can be simply presented as 'either/or' when it comes to evaluation and research. On one hand, do Circles put their energy into proving their worth through the blunt tool of statistical evidence, simply demonstrating reduction in reconviction rates, beloved of the hard-pressed policy maker and budget holder? Alternatively, do they present a wider frame, which reflects the original Mennonite principles in approaching the issues as wider social and community ones, in which we all must play our part and choose how to respond to those who have committed the most heinous of crimes, as viewed by society (see

Chapter 1)? This is to see those who have committed appalling crimes as individuals, as being, nevertheless, worthy and deserving of support through a humane reintegration back into their community.

In what some may feel to be a false polarity, the temptation can be to set the necessary reduction of reconvictions for sexual offences against a more overtly 'restorative' set of principles. These might also emphasise the rights of the offender to be given every assistance to rejoin society as a responsible, participating member.

Significant in this regard is a paper produced under the aegis of the 16th United Nations Commission on Crime Preventions and Criminal Justice, by Brown and Dandurand (2007). The authors present Circles as fundamentally having a community-engagement function and being primarily for the purpose of reintegrating offenders in their neighbourhoods. They stress Rule 46 of the European Rules on Community Sanctions and Measures, and the Guidelines for the Prevention of Crime, of the European Social Council 2002, where emphasis is laid on community participation in reducing reoffending. It may partly explain why, having come across the Circles model, colleagues in Holland and Belgium have been so quick to take it up.

One of the reasons one suspects that the research studies in Canada undertaken by Wilson and colleagues (2005, 2007a, 2007b) have been so respected is that they have successfully managed to use the perspectives of both crime reduction and broader community perception in the assessments of the Circles in that country.

Indeed, there are multiple risks in adopting a purely crime reduction approach to analysis. All too often, for instance, such data collection and interpretation are overly influenced by current policy needs. Jupp (1989) refers to the danger of 'what is seen as problematic is what is problematic for official policy' (p.22). This consideration will clearly dictate the drift of what is required and accepted as 'evidence'. In the current climate this can be seen in the government's increasing emphasis on 'payment by results'. This is being voiced in relation to the need to reduce prison places notably as short-term sentences are particularly associated with high rates of reoffending. Less clear is the period required over which results can be realistically assessed and therefore what interim measures for evaluation might be acceptable.

But an additional problem is highlighted by some researchers who note the actual absence of a clear theoretical foundation for any assessment of rehabilitative interventions. Ward and Maruna (2007) adopt a refreshingly honest approach in recognising that 'much of the blame for this lack of theoretical development, of course, lies with academic criminology' (p.28). They go on to quote Cullen (2002, p.283), who says, 'Although criminology is rich in categorizing theories of crime, true theories of correctional intervention are in short supply.' This at least provides Circles with some legitimacy in contributing to the debate as how best to measure what works and why. Fundamental to their exploration on rehabilitation is the recognition by Ward and Maruna (2007) that rehabilitation theory all too often asks what works as opposed to how it works. For many Circles it is a not uncommon experience for a core member, who has had more professional interventions than he would care to recall, to say at some point with grateful and poignant insight, 'This is the first time anyone has wanted to spend time with me, other than for the fact they are being paid for it.' There is an indication here perhaps as to 'how' one element of the Circles makes an impact, though not one easily categorised by the social scientist!

The background of rehabilitation

The therapeutic approach, in its widest and non-clinical sense with which the Circles model most closely identifies, is to be found in the Good Lives Model (see Chapter 3). Through this, crime and a range of psychological difficulties can be understood and appropriately viewed as maladaptive means for meeting common and shared human needs (Ward and Stewart 2003). But the development of the model can be seen in part as a response to what has been termed 'the reigning paradigm in rehabilitation', the Risk-Need-Responsivity model (Ward and Maruna 2007). This theory, it is suggested, has become the starting and end point for rehabilitative work in Europe and on the American continent. It focuses on the *dynamic risk factors*, which reflect criminogenic *needs*, resulting in acts of crime. Dynamic risk factors are changeable variables such as emotional states, which can fluctuate in response to a range of circumstances and stimuli. Static risk factors, however, are usually unchangeable, although there can be variation over a prolonged period of time, for example being reconvicted or establishing a significant and lasting relationship (Proulex *et al.* 2000). It makes sense, so the theory has it, therefore, to target resources according to the level of risk posed to the community, using the principle of 'responsivity', that is, managing the matching treatment and intervention with the learning style and other individual characteristics of the offender. But growing concerns with limitations of this model have been noted by a number of writers (Ward and Maruna 2007). While it is recognised that reducing dynamic risk factors is necessary, it is not of itself enough, and a broader range of rehabilitative resources is necessary related to improving well-being proactively as a goal in itself. It is also, critics suggest, a model which is limited through its assumption of 'one size fits all', which is insufficient to meet the complexities of true rehabilitative needs.

The Good Lives Model approaches with a different bias. Those convicted of sexual offences can be seen as having the same needs or 'primary goods' as everyone else – healthy living, control over their lives, a sense of purpose, and family relationships – and, while being monitored for public protection, can also be helped to acquire those goods more appropriately and without harm to others. The consonance here with the broader principles of restorative justice are self-evident and, for Circles with their weekly focus on assisting the core member to achieve the pro-social goals of their relapse prevention programme, the theoretical framework can direct the service objectives. Sex offender treatment programmes are increasingly drawing on the Good Lives Model and while Circles are not 'treatment' interventions themselves there is now a helpful and demonstrable continuity in approach and ethos. Ward and Maruna (2007), indeed, suggest that this overall approach should be extended to adjusting the everyday terminology of prisons and the probation service to reflect the Good Lives theory and principles, as the phrase 'relapse prevention' is negatively loaded and could more appropriately be framed as 'self-management' or 'change for life' – something this writer suspects Circles would enthusiastically endorse.

Theoretical, contextual and methodological challenges

Jupp (1989) neatly framed the balance of theory, context and methodology as the 'criminological enterprise'. This grouping may usefully serve to direct some of the questions behind any evaluation of Circles' impact. Part of the theoretical challenge in any evaluation lies in the approach to risk assessment, which is inevitably at the heart of referrals to Circles and their 'success' measures. Those individuals for whom Circles are sought are on the whole assessed as Level 2 or 3 according to the Multi-Agency Public Protection Agreements (see Chapter 3). As part of this assessment two standard tools are likely to have been used: the score on the Risk Matrix 2000 assessment for sex offenders (Hanson and Thornton 2000) and the OASys Risk of Serious Harm measure used by the statutory services. The former is an evidence-based risk-assessment tool using static factors for sex offenders, and the latter is a risk-analysis tool which assists in assessing offending-related needs and the likelihood of violent and non-violent reoffending.

Reliable evaluation and prediction assumes in the very first place a comprehensive and accurate availability of statistics on which theoreticians can build their models and suggest appropriate interventions. But as Jupp (1989) acknowledges, the gathering of accurate data in the field of criminology is fraught. Many criminal acts are unknown to the police and, if ever there was a field in which this was particularly true, then it must be that of sexual offending and particularly child sexual abuse, where 'secrets' abound and disclosure may not be for years, if ever.

In addition to the theoretical challenges for measuring the previously suggested 'what works', there are the practical problems of evaluation and research with which Circles must contend. Not least among these is distinguishing this community service from other interventions and contacts the core member may be enjoying. What is it that is unique about the Circles which can be legitimately claimed to be having a positive effect? A glib and ungenerous response to statutory and sometime voluntary sector partners might be that the reality is that relatively little is going on elsewhere, given the demands on hard-pressed public protection officers and their probation service colleagues. Certainly the annual report for Devon and Cornwall MAPPA (2010) acknowledged the additional and valuable 300 personal contacts with known sex offenders provided through the local Circles over and above those of the statutory agencies. Where volunteers regularly meet with core members for a social cup of coffee, a film or meal, over and beyond the weekly or fortnightly evening meetings, it would be perverse not to credit a distinct and influential contribution by the Circle.

Given context, the seeming polarity referred to above of retributive criminal justice and rehabilitative-restorative justice is fundamental. But evaluation of the service is of interest to a number of parties whose service priorities are not necessarily reflected in the simple distinction above. Besides the police and probation partners who have been the bedrock of Circles' development and often funding, there are voluntary sector partners who engage because they see Circles as meeting some of their corporate objectives. Barnardo's has a significant investment in the Northumbria Circles Project, as did the NSPCC until 2010 in Devon and Cornwall Circles. All of these agencies and a number of smaller, more local, partners might frame their primary motivation for involvement, and therefore evaluative objectives, somewhat differently. For Circles projects the challenge is keeping a wide focus, a similar consequence of having to provide different reports to multiple funders, all with differing priorities.

As the working context for the model is a formal arrangement between statutory partners such as police and probation and the local or national charities providing the Circles, further complexities can arise around understanding as to data protection in relation to the service delivery. Service level agreements between statutory partners and projects will detail the necessary and appropriate two-way flow of information. It is only relatively recently, however, that the implications of such data being used specifically for evaluation and research purposes, with the consent of core members, have fully been taken into account. The third of Jupp's elements of the criminological enterprise takes us into methodology, including the dynamics of quantitative and qualitative data collection.

With regards to quantitative analysis, the effectiveness of Circles as measured by the reduced reoffending of those ex-offenders attending a Circle cannot be judged by a simple comparison with offenders not attending a Circle. Circles participants have requested the support of a Circle and have been accepted as suitable core members. Their degree of motivation and commitment not to reoffend is, therefore, likely to be higher than for those not requesting support or those being rejected for support. The gold standard for research would be a randomised control trial in which offenders requesting and considered suitable for such engagement would be randomised either to receive that support or not. However, we consider that this would be unethical because there is already sufficient evidence that attending a Circle does reduce reoffending rates. The randomisation could, therefore, be predicted to disadvantage some offenders and result in otherwise avoidable future abuse. The comparisons must, therefore, be made using matched controls, as has been the case in the Canadian studies (Wilson *et al.* 2005, 2007a, 2007b). Each offender attending a Circle needs to be matched, ideally at the time of acceptance, with one or more offenders with as nearly equal as possible values of all those variables that are predictive of likely reoffending. Matching will not be possible on all the known predictive variables and these have to be recorded for future use in statistical analyses that attempt to adjust for such remaining differences.

Furthermore, contrary to popular belief, the relatively low reoffending rates of those convicted of sexual offences as a group, as opposed to other crime types, means that quantitative studies can be hard to populate.

The numbers of matched cases required to provide a statistically reliable cohort for any Circles impact study can take considerable time to accrue. Circles as a service in England and Wales are still two years short, at the time of writing, of the ten years the research purists would argue as vital for credible conclusions of effectiveness. The specific weakness of the absence in all of the matched control studies referred to above of a motivational variable to underpin comparison between the Circle-supported subject group and the control group can, however, be answered to some extent. First, that there was a degree of reoffending among those who experienced a Circle is clearly evidence that motivation is not all. Second, as already stated, the Canadian studies demonstrated less serious reoffending when it did occur among the Circle group, indicating a beneficial effect even when motivation not to reoffend failed.

In terms of qualitative data other challenges arise, but this has certainly proved the more accessible form in England and Wales in the first eight years of Circles. Through meeting notes of each weekly Circle, 'end of Circle summary reports', case studies, and volunteer feedback in supervision, a solid body of data is being assembled. The most structured approach is perhaps the Dynamic Risk Review tool (see below), undertaken by each Circle, minus the core member, on a quarterly basis, facilitated by their co-ordinator. However, such a qualitative method is entirely dependent upon volunteers, few of whom volunteered to engage in 'research' and for whom such a process borders on a bureaucratic irritation. A key challenge is achieving consistency of scoring by volunteers completing the review, though growing familiarity with the model and process will be especially helpful in overcoming this. This will be returned to below.

Summary of the 'evidence'

Having spent some time reviewing the background to evaluation and research of Circles, we are in position to consider what evidence there is to support the claims that they are effective. Few forms of service provision, especially in such a contentious and challenging arena as this, spring fully formed from Zeus's head, with a research plan attached, and baseline headings accurately anticipated as essential for use in five or ten years' time. The United Nations submission enthusiastically, albeit perhaps slightly prematurely in the case of the UK, referred to Circles as having 'been successfully implemented in Canada and England' (Brown and Dandurand 2007, p.3). Given that only one substantial piece of research had been conducted by this time, it was a bold statement. The case for the establishment of Circles in England and Wales was made across the Atlantic in Canada (see Chapter 1). It is in Canada, again, that to date the most rigorous and extensive research programmes have been undertaken. Studies by Wilson *et al.* (2005, 2007b), with carefully matched control groups, have now provided firm evidence that Circles do, indeed, reduce reoffending rates among those most likely to reoffend sexually and furthermore have a beneficial effect on the community's perceptions and feelings as to their own safety.

Besides the comparative reconviction results of those with sexual convictions who had the experience of a Circle as opposed to a matched control group who did not, Wilson *et al.* (2005) reviewed a wide range of impacts on those associated with Circles. The study elicited data on the Circle volunteers' belief as to the support felt by the core member, his ability to establish friendships and their sense of his increasing sense of self-worth. Scores were also secured for the core member's own sense of his acceptance by the volunteers and his perspective as to his position in the community. In the following study (Wilson *et al.*

2007a) information was sought about how the core members felt about being part of a Circle. Sixty-one per cent indicated they were 'proud' of this involvement. While such data does not necessarily meet many of the standards that would satisfy the Risk-Need-Responsivity purists, it clearly chimes with three of the Good Lives Model 'human goods' of self-directedness, inner peace and, indeed, happiness.

Partner agencies were also surveyed, with 93 per cent saying that after three years' involvement they still felt motivated to continue with the programme. This is certainly a reassuring finding that is reflected in the situation in England and Wales, where after eight years of growing Circles' partnerships in over 20 police and probation areas, not one partner agency has withdrawn citing a lack of confidence in the model and its effectiveness.

With regard to reduction in reoffending rates, Wilson *et al.* (2005) carefully matched two groups of 45 men each with serious sexual offending histories, one group of which had experienced a Circle for three and a half years and one which had not. Besides offering evidence of a reoffending rate of 70 per cent less than the non-Circle control group, those who did reoffend from the group who had enjoyed Circle support committed less serious offences than their original conviction had been for prior to incarceration.

The later study (Wilson *et al.* 2007a) again took a broad approach to the impact and experience of Circles, looking at the perspectives of core members, volunteers and professionals. While some interesting and useful data was elicited from professional partners as to their concerns about the ability of volunteers always to maintain boundaries, and some weak structures, 70 per cent (N=16) of those professionals interviewed reported that 'what they liked most about COSA [Circles of Support and Accountability] was that they increase offender responsibility and accountability, and that community safety was the focus (63 per cent)' (p.299).

Wilson *et al.* (2007b) this time looked at two groups of 60 men each and once again saw a marked reduction in reoffending rates for the group with Circle engagement as opposed to the matched group without. The matching had been done against the General Statistical Information on Recidivism scale (GSIR) with recidivism being understood as a charge for a new sexual offence or for the breaking of a condition applied by the court. The reduction represented a figure lower by 25 per cent than would be expected from the actuarial recidivism rates projected for this group, given their matched variables. For the authors of this study, 'This result underscores the ultimate position that COSA have a marked, positive effect on the community integration and long-term functioning of high-risk sexual offenders released at Warrant Expiry Date' (see Chapter 1) and they noted that 'the comparison group have been responsible for considerably more mayhem in the community than their COSA counterparts' (Wilson *et al.* 2007b, p.334).

In their conclusion to their report on the replication of outcome findings Wilson *et al.* (2009), reviewing the highly favourable reduction of reoffending rates of their COSA participants, as against the matched control group, categorically make the theoretical and evidential connection with both the RNR foundations and the Good Lives Model. They say, 'The COSA approach is, therefore, fully in line with the risk and need elements of the principles of effective intervention…as well as the tenets of the Good Lives Model' (p.426).

Closer to home, in 2007 the Hampshire and Thames Valley Circles Project reviewed 16 men who had experienced Circles (Bates *et al.* 2007). Of these, nine displayed high-risk behaviours reported to the police by the volunteers, thereby preventing a further offence, with four of those men being recalled to prison, and the remainder managed in the community.

A further and more recent study by Bates *et al.* (under review) has been undertaken by HTV Circles, which as one of the early Circles pilot projects now has a substantial body of data on which to report. The results of this small-scale study are very positive in demonstrating not only an impressively low rate of reconviction for sexual offences among the 60 core members reviewed, but also successful pro-social gains and achievements on the part of the cohort members. The average period of follow-up was 36.2 months, with 25 of the 60 above the average figure. Just one reconviction for a sexual offence was recorded (and verified through the Police National Computer data) and this, it was noted, was for downloading images of child abuse, as opposed to the cause of the original conviction which had been for sustained contact offences against three children. This is not to minimise the seriousness of downloading but, as indicated in the Canadian studies, a less immediately harmful consequence was noted in the new offence. There is of course no randomised control trial data here and the authors are wary of lodging definitive claims, but they are confident in asserting that 70 per cent of those reviewed provided evidence that the well-being of the core member had improved and that this could be attributed to the Circle involvement. The Good Lives Model would credit this as being a key component in contributing to positive rehabilitation.

A wider-ranging study is now underway in England and Wales, in conjunction with the University of Leeds, commissioned by Circles UK, the umbrella charity for all Circles projects. Through funding provided by the Wates Charitable Foundation, a review of the work of the past eight years is being undertaken and this will provide a qualitative and, to some degree, quantitative study. Interviews with a range of core members, volunteers, staff and relevant partner agencies will provide invaluable data concerning perspectives as to the impact of Circles in the broad context demonstrated by Wilson in Canada. Reconviction rates of those who have been through a Circle here will be compared with data on matched individuals drawn from prison records with key variables matched or recorded for later adjustments, and with data from the Police National Computer for information on reconvictions across the non-Circle control group, as well as for core members.

It would be tempting to leave it there as 'case proved' for Circles. However, there is a further methodological challenge in distinguishing between what exactly can be attributed to the Circle's engagement or that of any other agency. This is becoming an even more contentious question in the light of the government's growing emphasis on 'payment by results' and the anticipated funding streams through 'social investors' who will contract with providers on the basis of evident savings in criminal justice costs, notably associated with custodial sentences. Where a provider subcontracts to another agency specialising in one element of the rehabilitative work, the devil will truly be in the detail when attempting to lay claim to which service made the critical and ameliorative difference.

Internal evaluation

This takes us to one of the internal evaluation systems that have been developed by Circles UK in England and Wales, not initially with regard to funding and subcontracting, but that does serve to concentrate the mind. The Dynamic Risk Review tool, referred to above, emerged from an appreciation on the part of Circles UK that a more structured regular means for measuring the effectiveness of a Circle was required. While minutes of weekly or fortnightly Circle gatherings were kept by the volunteers, quarterly reviews logged and records made at the conclusion of a Circle, it was felt that much data was collected but was not being used in any form to evaluate outcomes formally.

The Dynamic Risk Review was determined as a basis for a more structured evaluation as to a core member's progress, or lack thereof, in the four 'domains' of the Structured Assessment of Risk and Need (SARN). The SARN, developed by the Prison Service in 2005, and for which permission was sought and kindly agreed for this more modest usage by Circles, is a process for assessing risk, treatment needs and progress in those convicted of sexual offences. Some models for assessing sex offender risk only make use of static factors, that is, the ones largely unchanging over time, while dynamic risk factors, such as emotional states, have tended to receive less attention than their static counterparts. The frequency and regularity with which four or five Circles volunteers will meet with their core member far exceeds that possible to the hard-pressed offender manager who is also likely to be conducting his or her interview in a very different ambience and in a more formally prescribed direction.

But Circle projects accumulate a considerable body of information of a dynamic nature in relation to the core member who will often, so experience proves, tell his group of volunteers things about himself and life not shared with professional agencies for possible fear of the consequences.

The Dynamic Risk Review, therefore, needed to achieve a number of objectives. It had to:

- elicit in a structure but enabling manner information indicating change in dynamic risk factors
- provide a dependable scoring means for tracking changes over a period of time
- ensure that scores allocated can be justified, by giving examples
- be sufficiently thorough without placing an undue demand on Circles volunteers.

The final point was referred to earlier and acknowledges the challenge of getting volunteers to undertake this process, when they did not join the programme to engage in the regular filling-out of evaluation forms. Besides a constitutional resistance to such 'bureaucracy' as perceived by a proportion of otherwise dedicated volunteers, there would be a practical and logistical hurdle as to how and when the form might be completed. Precious volunteer time is best used in face-to-face contact with the core member, and an additional evening in a week or a prolonged meeting beyond the core member's departure could well prove a form too far. This was also not a logistical problem confined to the volunteers as a pilot exercise demonstrated that the forms were most reliably, consistently and comprehensively completed when done with the assistance of the project co-ordinator. They, too, would have had a long day and given the geographical spread of Circles might well find themselves travelling home some considerable distance late at night after a review had been completed.

The benefits of the model, if it could be made to work, were acknowledged to be:

- a growing body of data collected by the same group of individuals over a period of time about perceived changes in dynamic risk factors

- ability to compare collected data at different stages of a Circle, notably beginning and end

- scope to compare scores and data as to specific dynamic risk factors concerning core members

- scope to identify trends and thereby possible weaknesses and strengths in Circles process.

The pilot exercise which tested out the form and process produced some invaluable lessons. One pilot relied on volunteers in a Circle completing and submitting the form independently of each other. The other was a collective exercise assisted by the co-ordinator. The latter was by far the more 'successful' not only in terms simply of the work being completed and provided on time, but also in the quality of anecdotal examples given to support specific scores. Initial and understandable resistance from some volunteers was expected, and they did not disappoint! However, it was accurately anticipated that this was more likely to be the case for those volunteers who were used to operating without such a process on a quarterly basis, whereas for new volunteers the review could be introduced as standard. Indeed, the review now features as an expectation of practice and is an integral part of the volunteer training programme, with explanation as to its value in eliciting data, which with other benefits is also invaluable in furnishing evidence for income generation.

As yet it is too early to be able to make meaningful statements as to what trends can be seen through the completed reviews coming in; the understanding being that once they have been collected for a year – four reports on a core member – Circles UK will then provide an analysis to each project. As this corpus develops, the comparisons between projects and collective material can be assessed and hopefully some coherent and defensible conclusions drawn.

But there is no suggestion that this is the SARN in practice in a community context, because it is conducted by untrained volunteers. All the project co-ordinators were trained before the review was implemented, but the completion is dependent upon volunteers and in that lies both weakness and strength. On the one hand there can be a lack of 'professional rigour', but there are also the advantages of a commonsense judgement by community members who may have accumulated much experience of direct engagement with, and sensitivity to, those who have sexual convictions. There is a recognition therefore that claims of the 'effectiveness' of Circles in reducing risk drawn from reviews must be tested against other evaluative methods, and thus honour the principle of triangulation of methodology in research.

However, what has become clear through responses from volunteers is that they are now finding the review to be a helpful and focused method for stepping back on a regular basis, comparing notes and reviewing what differences they can reasonably identify in the core member's behaviour and attitudes. With the principle of 'no secrets' being central to Circles, ensuring that the core member is aware of the most recent reflections and scores can be hugely affirming but also used as a creative challenge to perceived concerns.

In researching and evaluating the work of Circles the perennial matter of who pays the piper calls the tune is never far away. The central dynamic as to whether Circles are a model for enhancing community reintegration of those with histories of sexual offending or primarily a crime-reduction intervention in an area which is notoriously challenging to manage, remains influential, not least in how to set about measuring what to do and if, and equally importantly, how it works.

The national financial crisis, which has endowed the phrase 'payment by results' in the field of criminal justice with increased importance, will undoubtedly influence the direction of research. Indeed it may be that the 'pathways' of the Home Office Reducing Re-offending National Action Plan 2004, to which HTV Circles point in its study (Bates *et al.* 2011), provide an increasingly fruitful conceptual framework for continuing evaluation and longer-term research. Measurements of the pathway progress of individuals, such as in relation to housing, drugs and alcohol and family support network developments, could provide specific data which accumulatively strengthens the evidence of the Circles model and justifies financial support. Such an approach would also carry the added benefit of being entirely comfortable alongside the principled Good Lives Model, with which Circles already have such an affinity.

Chapter 7

Publish and Damn

THE MEDIA AND SEX OFFENDING

Terry Philpot

Mods and rockers throwing deckchairs and beer bottles at one another in Clacton, Brighton and other British seaside resorts during Whitsun and Easter bank holiday weekends in 1964 now seem a lifetime away. Indeed, those who participated in what now appear to have been no more than street fights, albeit involving large numbers of people, are now grandparents, most of them very likely respectable and retired citizens.

Yet the passage of the 39 years since Cohen (1972) used those events to formulate his ideas about 'folk devils' and 'moral panics' has done nothing to diminish the relevance of what he said. Drugs, the behaviour of some young people, immigrants and asylum seekers, and single mothers have their unwanted periodic bursts of media coverage as they have been lined up to exemplify the threat to social order, diminishing moral standards, and, indeed, a generalised threat by The Other.[7]

Criticism of the use of the concept of moral panics is that it simplifies issues. Nevertheless, some of its key characteristics – volatility, social concern and awareness of the danger, the hostility towards a group, and the disproportionate response – have proven a durably helpful way of understanding responses to certain events and how these 'threats' are constructed. Indeed, what is particularly helpful is that far from the concept simplifying the issue, it can illustrate how the construction and response to a subject can result in a more simplistic view of an issue and, in so doing, place obstacles in the way of solving the problem.

Nowhere is this more so than in the media portrayal of child sex offenders.[8] This is not to say that this portrayal does not indicate genuine public concern. The wish to protect children is a healthy and responsible one and it is understandable that local communities can sometimes react adversely to a hostel for former offenders being placed in their area, especially when there has been no meaningful consultation.

But if a moral panic implies a collective reaction, the media can also induce what one might call low-key, individual negative reactions towards offenders that filter into political and public discourse. The media presents the ever-threatening, omnipresent 'perv', 'monster', 'beast' and 'paedo' and his offending with the implication that no child is safe, that strangers are to be avoided. The facts – that most abuse is carried out by family members or those known and trusted by the child – are avoided. This distortion is presented in ways characteristic of how moral panics are constructed and stimulated and how they affect the perceptions of both individuals and groups. Here, the sex offender is a 'folk devil'.

While press coverage of child abuse is not a modern phenomenon (Kitzinger 2004, pp.33–4), in the past two or so decades there has been a 'rediscovery' which has enhanced public consciousness about the issue.[9] How extensive this coverage has been is evidenced by Kitzinger (1996), who found that, for example, *The Times* increased its reporting by 300 per cent between 1985 and 1987.

Child protection touches a nerve in our society for very understandable reasons: children are society's most vulnerable; they are seen as innocent; they represent, and are, the future. They rely on adults – their family, neighbours, and professionals such as teachers – for guidance, protection and sustenance. They need adults to fulfil their physical and emotional needs. Thus, the sexual abuse of a child is to take advantage of their vulnerability and trust, and, literally, to violate their innocence. How we, as a society, act and react to the sexual abuse of children is, in an important part, influenced by media coverage, but such coverage is also a reflection of our own feelings and cultural norms. For example, how we deal with crimes against children is seen in different ways. One of these is through denial and shifting the blame. Those who abuse children are not 'us' or those close to 'us' but 'the stranger'. Telling children not to talk to strangers is well ingrained in our culture for just this reason. In fact, while we know that children are more likely to be abused by family members and others whom they know and trust, for many people – and certainly for the tabloid press – this is knowledge too far. 'Stranger danger' looms so large partly because the most egregious crimes which come to public attention – the abduction and murder of Sarah Payne in 2000 is the most obvious – are often carried out by strangers. Their comparative rarity, and the drama which attends them, is what brings them to the front pages.

The abducted child is, in newspaper terms, a 'good' story. It has the element of the unknown – who did it, where and how? – and the story often runs for some while because of new leads, fresh witnesses appearing, reported sightings of the child or her abduction, and periodic reports by the police of their progress. Appeals by relatives, in obvious distress, and with cameras clicking away, add to this drama. It (rightly) unites all parents, indeed the public, in a community of concern – what if that had been *my* child? – with the attendant hopes raised for a safe return and apprehension of the perpetrator. In contrast, abuse in the family home is far less dramatic and also something which some newspapers – particularly self-described 'family newspapers' – are less inclined to inflict upon their readers.

Why does the media act as it does?

A study from the United States by Chiet (2003), while admittedly very small and very local, but nevertheless meticulously researched, is very instructive in confirming wider patterns of how the media reacts to aspects of abuse. He looked at what determined whether a story was covered. He analysed two databases over five years. The first identified all defendants charged with 'child molestation' in Rhode Island in 1993. The second was created by electronic searching of the *Providence Journal* for every story that mentioned each defendant.

Cheit found that most (56.1%) of the defendants were not mentioned in the newspaper. However, factors which determined a greater chance of coverage included cases of the first degree; those with multiple counts; those involving additional violence or multiple victims; and those leading to a long prison sentence. 'The data indicate that the press exaggerates "stranger danger", while intra-familial cases are underreported' are among the author's conclusions.

Some of what Chiet says is confirmed by a much larger study by (among others) Kitzinger and Skidmore (1995) (quoted by Kitzinger

2004). They found that 96 per cent of newspaper articles about how to protect children focus on threats from strangers, while only 4 per cent are concerned about the most common threat of all – that from male relatives. The authors also noted the sparse attention accorded by the media to prevention.

The media is also concerned to show that crimes against children by strangers are common. When the bodies of Holly Wells and Jessica Chapman were found in 2002, the *Daily Mail* editorial stated:

> [This] is no isolated nightmare. Such horrors occur almost every year, each raising the anguished question: 'How could this happen again?'

Here is a good, but not isolated, example that promotes the idea that no child is safe and that you cannot afford to take your eyes off a child for a moment. Such attitudes make us more inward-looking and overly protective towards children, and morbidly suspicious of others and their motives. But it also makes us believe that if we keep children away from strangers, or at least wary of them, then all will be well. This misplaced emphasis is not only unnecessarily alarmist, it also distorts the real picture.

Those who write the stories may also be influenced by their ambivalence about abuse. This may simply be the common disbelief or denial that many people have, that such things cannot be done to children by members of their family or people they know and trust, or at least cannot be done on the scale claimed.

Journalists may also be influenced by other considerations. Take, for example, the well-rehearsed media portrayal of social workers in any number of child protection cases. In this the social worker is attacked for taking children away from their parents but also blamed, when something goes wrong, for not doing so. They have become 'middle class folk devils', says Cohen (2002), 'either gullible wimps or else storm troopers of the nanny state; either uncaring or cold-hearted bureaucrats…or else over-zealous, do-gooding meddlers.' How can the social worker win? Even the best intentioned reporter is not a social worker. He or she maybe cannot be expected to understand the dilemmas faced by those who are charged with assessing risks to children and with the power to remove them from their families. And those reporters in search of a sensational story may not even care what the truth is.

Another factor which may create ambivalence is the miscarriages of justice that have occurred in child sex abuse cases. These are sometimes the result of massive police investigations into historic abuse, where arrests can be secured by trawling, the lure of financial compensation for victims, convictions gained by offers of pardons to people in prison, and the change in the law which allows uncorroborated evidence in court. Sometimes miscarriages of justice are related to so-called 'false memory syndrome' where statements – primarily by women – occur that they were abused by their fathers or other male relatives and, now in adulthood, often through therapy, have recovered a memory of the abuse. Sometimes such claims gain media attention and may play a part in creating a belief that accusations of abuse are unreliable or, at least, that claims of abuse are exaggerated.

Naming and shaming: On the streets and in the editors' offices

The *News of the World*'s 'naming and shaming' campaign is the most notorious example of the influence of the media in child sex abuse cases, partly because of the disturbances it provoked. It stands as a prime example of moral panic with regard to sex offenders. In the wake of the death of Sarah Payne, the newspaper said it would publish the names, addresses, details and photographs of an alleged 110,000 sex offenders in order, it claimed, to further public protection. In the event, the newspaper published information on 50 alleged offenders in its issues of 23 and 30 July 2000. The *News of the World* admitted that some of the names were gleaned from Scout Association records, which themselves had been, in part, compiled from local newspapers. On 3 August, the *Daily Mirror* gave its support to the campaign, an unusual step for a newspaper owned by a different publisher. The headlines accompanying the stories and photographs give a vivid flavour of the campaign's tone: 'DOES A MONSTER LIVE NEAR YOU?' and 'WHAT TO DO IF THERE IS A PERVERT ON YOUR DOORSTEP'. Some professional groups, notably the Association of Chief Police Officers and the National Association of Probation Officers, came out in opposition to the campaign, fearing that offenders would go underground. The campaign was, however, supported by Sarah Payne's parents.

In August, Paulsgrove, an area of Portsmouth, made the national and international news as mobs, marching with children and carrying placards, attacked the homes of suspected and actual sex offenders. Small children were reported to have chanted, 'Sex case, sex case – hang 'em, hang 'em, hang 'em' (McCartney 2000). Police were drafted in to protect offenders or those suspected of being such when each night for a week up to 300 people marched on local homes. In one instance a mob of 150 people was reported to have gathered outside the home of a woman whose brother had been convicted of offences in the 1980s. 'You perve' was daubed on the windows of the house. The brother had not lived there for 15 years (McCartney 2000). On another occasion, local people damaged the home of a woman who was a *paediatrician*. Five homes were wrecked and there were 35 arrests.

The residents had a list of names culled from newspapers and hearsay and were demanding that the council move those on the list from the estate. Five families were subsequently removed although the police said that none had any connection with sex offences (McCartney 2000).

In this lamentable episode Syd Rapson, then MP for Portsmouth North, the constituency in which Paulsgrove lay, played what might be considered a less than helpful part. He had lived on the Paulsgrove estate for 30 years and spoke of 'democracy having its way', adding, 'I sympathise with the initial aims of the democratic protest but not with any attached violence' (Milmo 2000a). However, he was also quoted as saying that the events were 'nothing more than a latter day witch-hunt' (Milmo 2000b).

Later, he said, 'We want the residents to provide the names they have, and in return those on it will be advised it is in their interest to move. It is far from ideal but if this is the victory that the campaigners need to stop their protests then so be it' (Milmo 2000a).

However, on 4 August the *News of the World*, without admitting that this was the reason, was forced to end its naming and shaming when it was revealed that at least four men had been wrongly identified and attacked by vigilantes.

This sort of 'naming and shaming' coverage demonstrates a lack of responsibility, which, to judge by what they say, some newspaper executives are unconcerned about, bearing out Prime Minister Stanley Baldwin's remark that the power of the press was 'the prerogative of the harlot throughout the ages – power without responsibility'.

The then editor of the *News of the World*, Rebekah Wade (now Brooks), never gave an interview about her policies. However, Silverman and Wilson (2002) quote a short but enlightening interview with the public relations manager for the *News of the World*, Hayley Barlow, conducted by Sonia Millington, a master's student in criminal justice policy at the University of Central England, in November 2000:

> Q: Were you aware of the potential dangers that the [naming and shaming] campaign could cause?
>
> A: Oh, yes, very much so.
>
> Q: Do you feel any responsibility for the vigilante attacks that occurred as a result of the campaign?
>
> A: We don't take any responsibility in the sense that, right from the word 'go', our core objective with this campaign was to warn, to alert but definitely not to incite. Unfortunately, in this country…there are a handful of people who see fit to take the law into their own hands. All the attacks that took place, bar one [that one being against Victor Burnett at Paulsgrove], were mistaken identity and people who we had not named and shamed in the newspapers.
>
> Q: So you don't take any responsibility for the violence?
>
> A: No.

Wade's own justification was summed up in her editorial, headed 'For Sarah', which announced the naming and shaming campaign:

> There are 110,000 sex offenders in Britain…one for every square mile. The murder of Sarah Payne has proved police monitoring of these perverts is not enough. So we are revealing WHO they are and WHERE they are…starting today.
>
> (quoted in Cross 2005, p.288)

In fact, the *News of the World* was not there first. Kitzinger (2004) reports an earlier case, occasioned by another naming and shaming campaign, when a young girl died after the house in which she was staying was burned down. In Birmingham, the 81-year-old mother of a convicted sex offender was forced to flee her home.

And on 12 July 2000, two weeks before the national newspaper launched its campaign, the *Peterborough Evening Telegraph* ran a story about 67-year-old Billy Baker who had been sentenced to three years' probation for indecently assaulting four girls (Silverman and Wilson 2002). A neighbour had tipped off the press – there had been no court coverage – because they thought the sentence too lenient and that Baker had not figured in the name and shame list being run in the newspaper.

Under a protocol with the local media, the police supplied details of court hearings not attended by the local press whereby journalists were given information to set matters in context – for example, the seriousness of the offence or whether a conviction was spent. In this case, the police warned the newspaper that there could be serious consequences were the details to be published.

The next day the headline proclaimed 'The enemy within', with a picture of Baker, his address and comments by one of his victim's grandparents that she would 'kill' him if she got hold of him. Within hours, posters appeared on lamp-posts with his photograph and address. Crowds gathered where Baker lived and the police took him to a safe house.

On 13 July, Kevin Booth, the newspaper's editor, defended himself in a leader article where he equated the naming and shaming of sex offenders with publishing the names and addresses of TV licence dodgers. The newspaper also published a reader poll purporting to have 88 per cent of readers backing their efforts to run Baker out of town. It is known that 90 people responded to the poll, when the newspaper boasts a 24,000 circulation (Silverman and Wilson 2002, pp.163–5).

Another example of irresponsibility of a different kind was demonstrated by Jim McDowell, editor of the *Belfast Sunday World*. He explained to Greer (2003) that when the Probation Board of Northern Ireland, with whom his newspaper shared a building, castigated him for calling offenders 'monsters', he told them:

> Survivors of sex crime call them fucking monsters, and I
> said that we are the newspaper these people come to and if
> they call them monsters, we'll call them monsters, it's dead
> simple. (p.138)

In this statement, and in Wade's editorial quoted above, each offence and offender is indistinguishable from another – they are all lumped together. Cross (2005) points out that only about 50 of the 110,000 convicted sex offenders fall into the category of predatory 'paedophiles', as he calls them. In such coverage, however, the media bundles all offenders together, without distinction, and with no regard to the varying severity of their crimes or their ability to manage their behaviour.

Wade's concern, in her response to the Sarah Payne murder, took as its theme the need for a British version of Megan's Law in the USA, whereby, in some states, the names and addresses of offenders living in an area are publicly notified. While the newspaper did bring an early end to its campaign, it could be judged to have had a partial success with the introduction of 'Sarah's Law'. This allows those with a legitimate concern to find out from the police if someone has a history of sex offending. It was implemented in eight police force areas in August 2010, having been piloted in another four.

The media and government two-step

In some cases politicians' collusion with irresponsible media coverage has given it validity. Silverman and Wilson (2002) draw specific attention, for instance, to the part played in the *News of the World*'s 'naming and shaming' campaign by the then Home Secretary Jack Straw.

Straw had received from Wade a letter setting out her proposals for strengthening public protection. Silverman and Wilson (2002) detail the internal furore in the Home Office caused by the Secretary of State's anxiety to reply by return of post. Yet he was unable to find time to talk to police and probation services in the areas where disturbances against alleged offenders were taking place. Gill Mackenzie, one-time chief probation officer in Gloucestershire and spokesperson on sex offending for the Association of Chief Officers of Probation, said:

> There were times during meetings when Rebekah Wade talked of the Home Secretary as though he was a puppet whom she could manipulate. In fact, there was something frighteningly contemptuous of politicians and democracy as a whole in the *News of the World*'s attitude.
>
> (quoted in Silverman and Wilson 2002, p.154)

Research by Davidson (2008) led her to conclude that there was collusion between the government and the paper. 'It is clear…that the government had been discussing both the proposed trip [to the United States by Gerry Sutcliffe, a Home Officer minister, to see if Megan's Law could be implemented in the UK] and possible measures to control sex offenders with the *News of the World* well in advance of informing Parliament' (p.89). This was six years after the 'naming and shaming' campaign.

Another example of the apparent intimidation of politicians by the media is provided by the events surrounding the release on parole in 1997 of Robert Oliver, followed a year later by Sidney Cooke. Both were notorious and very dangerous predatory child sex offenders, imprisoned as part of a gang, for the rape and manslaughter of 14-year-old Jason Swift. They were also suspected of other murders. One witness against them was another gang member, Leslie Bailey, who had been murdered by fellow prisoners while incarcerated. In 1991, the Crown Prosecution Service had declined to pursue prosecution for the alleged murders mentioned by Bailey because Cooke was already serving a long sentence. Demonstrations took place outside the prison even before Cooke was released.

The two men were not together but the media was chasing them – they were moving around the country and local newspapers were reporting alleged sightings, a favourite practice of local newspapers to give national stories a local dimension. Oliver sought police protection, which he later found in a medium secure unit near Milton Keynes. Cooke gained his sanctuary in a suite of police cells in Yeovil but was later charged, convicted and sentenced for other offences.[10]

Both the probation service and the police were worried about the release of these men into the community and the lack of suitable facilities in which to house them. No minister took part in the debate to explain what the facts were. And when Tony Butler, then chief constable in Gloucestershire and spokesperson on sex offending for the Association of Chief Probation Officers, sent a letter to the appropriate Home Office minister, he did not receive even the courtesy of a response (Silverman and Wilson 2002).

It is clear that when it comes to the coverage of sex offenders, we have the press acting irresponsibly alongside politicians who, at best, are being manipulated by the media and, at worst, are colluding with this hysteria-inducing coverage.

The government's silence over the *News of the World* campaign may have been occasioned, as Silverman and Wilson (2002) suggest, by fears that any statements would be attacked as a threat to press freedom. It is just as likely that the then government saw any contrary view as a potential vote-loser and possibly damaging to their carefully cultivated relationship with the Murdoch press.

Interestingly, while the *News of the World* campaign was only two years past and the media was evoking new dangers following the terrible deaths in August 2002 of Jessica Chapman and Holly Wells, the Home Office was offering initial funding for the first Circles (see Chapter 1). This is proof that what is said (or not said) publicly does not always reflect the actions of government. (However, even that positive decision was not without its media backlash: 'What a waste of our cash', a *Sunday Express* headline informed its readers in 2002, over the by-line of Robert Kilroy-Silk, the MEP and former television presenter.)

The effect on public attitudes and understanding

Paulsgrove is the most obvious example of the shaping of public opinion. This is an extreme example but it does illustrate that the way in which such cases are reported – with the emphasis on the more sensational ones, stereotypical depictions of offenders, the concentration on 'stranger danger' and the use of derogatory language to describe those convicted – shapes public understanding of sex offending. Most important, it detracts from practical, positive ways of dealing with the issue and thus from offering real and effective protection for children.

Taking all of this together – sensationalism, stereotypes, omissions, alarmist stories, language – it is not surprising that we see the scenes we do outside courts, in front of the homes of alleged sex offenders, or even the occasional murder of, or assault on, sex offenders who have been released from prison and, in some cases, men killed after being mistaken for an offender.

The media has become far more intrusive and irresponsible in the last two or three decades. The press, as it existed until the 1970s, is almost unrecognisable. Too many local newspapers now follow the generally sensationalist approach of their tabloid big brothers when it comes to crime reporting. However, in the case of sex offending, there is, in fact, evidence to show the naming and shaming began with local and regional newspapers and was later adopted by the national press (Critcher 2002; Cross 2005; Kitzinger 2004).

As Kitzinger (2004, p.108) has pointed out, the public are not passive, not 'dry sponges uncritically absorbing all that they see and hear'. We bring to our reading and viewing our own prejudices, experiences, reactions, outlooks and those other factors which make us, intellectually and emotionally, who we are.

Kitzinger concludes that audiences are more diverse than they are often given credit for but adds:

> Nevertheless, my research reveals that in spite of, and sometimes *because* [her emphasis] of this, the media are a crucial resource in constructing our sense of the world around us. The mass media can help to define what counts as a public issue, impact upon our understandings of individual cases, shape suspicions and beliefs, and resource memories and conversations. (p.180)

The media is part of a wider society. It both shapes and is shaped by that society. Discussion of sex – positive and negative – is a staple of the media. Our society is one that frequently treats sex as a cause for titillation, as a commodity, as a means to sell products, and is one that will exploit children for commercial purposes. The sexualisation of children through products aimed at them is one of the most worrying traits of the last decade.[11]

Paulsgrove, and similar manifestations elsewhere, were linked to media coverage. They were extreme examples and did, at times, resemble the age of public hanging, bear baiting and going to watch the inmates of the asylum. But extreme manifestations arising from saturation media coverage does not mean that all is well at other times. The gradual drip in the way court cases are often reported, as well as stories of missing children and the style of their reporting, also influences public perceptions, far less dramatically, but also with negative consequences. This has a cumulative effect: the stories which influence our thinking may be forgotten or half remembered with the passage of time, but what remains is the *impression* that we have of offenders.

We should remember – to understand, not to excuse – that those reporting crimes of a sexual nature may be specialist crime or court reporters for national newspapers. On local newspapers, they are almost certain to be general reporters. They have no special knowledge about offending or offenders. They are also ordinary people, subject to the prejudices and assumptions of the rest of the population, not informed by any specialist knowledge.

Both types of coverage – the much rarer, sensationalist 'naming and shaming' and the more low-level, everyday reporting – create a view of the 'otherness' of the offender, that he and his offences are elsewhere, and that what he does happens to other people.

Such responses distance us from sex offenders: we see them as less than human. Indeed, the frequently used tabloid words 'monster' and 'beast' actually suggest that they are just that. And the more we see them in this light, the less we will be able to understand why they acted as they did and to view them as people who can be helped to manage their behaviour, and, by so doing, save children from the terrible consequences of their actions.

Endnotes

1. We have very deliberately avoided using the word 'paedophile' because it is misleadingly inaccurate. It is often taken generally to refer to someone who is sexually interested in prepubescent children, which itself says nothing about the age difference between the two parties. It also ignores the fact that the behaviours of child sex offenders are so varied and, too, is taken to mean that those defined as such are only sexually interested in children. This ignores the many offenders who engage in sexual activity with both children and adults (see Chapter 2). The association of the word with psychiatry can also imply those who are 'paedophiles' are in some way mentally abnormal by comparison with what are regarded as other norms of sexual behaviour

   Cossins' (2000) definition of a sex offender is useful. This is a 'man or male [*sic* but see note 2 below] adolescent who engages in contact or non-contact sexual activities with a child for the purposes of obtaining sexual gratification and who is: (i) at least five years older than the child; or (ii) younger, the same age as the child, or between one and four years older than the child in circumstances where the sexual activity was non-consensual.'

2. According to Grubin (1998), fewer than five per cent of those who sexually offend against children are women, often in association with men. The figures may be higher according to population studies, and Bunting (2005) attributes this to the possibility that professional lack of awareness and training may hide the figures.

   Hampshire and Thames Valley Circles has had two Circles for women and the Lucy Faithfull Foundation has had one Circle for a woman.

3. For the only substantial study of the partners of sex offenders, see Philpot (2009).

4. More than a third (36%) of recorded rapes are committed against children under 16 years of age (Walker, Kershaw and Nicholas 2006). Lovell (2002) refers to 'a broad consensus' that estimates that between 25 and 35 per cent of abusers are young people, mainly adolescent males. Stuart and Baines (2004) quote Home Office statistics that show that 1.6 per cent of convictions and cautions in 2001 were of women.

5. Finkelhor's (1984) pre-conditions have been helpfully tabulated by Sanderson (2004, see table 3.1, pp.94–5).

6. For a vivid description of the problems faced by Wolvercote and its demise, see Niechcial (2010).

7. Folk devils and moral panics, if not so called, have, of course, a much longer history. Arthur Miller's *The Crucible*, set in Puritan Massachusetts, is a portrayal of the panic about witchcraft at that time and a parable for the 'Red scares' of early 1950s America. Silverman and Wilson (2002) give an interesting potted history of some past British moral panics, while Cole (2003) shows how fear of trades unions, socialism and immigrants – often inextricably intertwined – has shaped American consciousness historically and today influences the 'war on terror'.

8. Television soaps, too, have taken up the themes of abuse. *EastEnders*, *Emmerdale* and *Coronation Street* all ran such plots in 2010, but only the first of these – in fact, the second time it had featured such a plot – was about sexual abuse; the other two concerned physical abuse. *Brookside* had a two-year storyline from 1993 to 1994. The role of television, though, is a separate issue and one outside of the remit of this chapter.

9. The media alone was not responsible for this greater awareness. For example, in October 1986 ChildLine (not wholly concerned with abuse) was launched.

10. Cooke was convicted of other sexual crimes committed in 1972 and 1973 and received two life sentences. He remains in prison today at the age of 84.

11. One of the most extraordinary blind spots about children portrayed as sex objects was seen when *Yes, Prime Minister*, based on the popular 1980s television comedy series, came to the London stage in 2010–11. It played for six months to sell-out audiences and was later revived. Few critics – Mark Lawson, in the Catholic weekly *The Tablet*, was an honourable exception – remarked on the distasteful central plot device. This involved the consequences for the signing of a trade agreement if an Eastern European leader, visiting London, was not supplied with an under-age virgin. Some members of the audience were said to have walked out.

References

Bates, A., Falshaw, L., Corbett C., Patel, V. and Friendship, C. (2004) 'A follow-up study of sex offenders treated by the Thames Valley sex offender group work programme 1995–1999.' *Journal of Sexual Aggression 29*, 29–38.

Bates, A., Macrae, R., Webb, C. and Williams, D. (2011) 'Ever-increasing Circles: A descriptive study of Hampshire and Thames Valley Circles of Support and Accountability 2002–2009.' *Journal of Sexual Aggression.* DOI: 10.1080/13552600.2010.544415.

Bates, A., Saunders, R. and Wilson, C. (2007) 'Doing something about it: A follow-up study of sex offenders participating in Thames Valley Circles of Support and Accountability.' *British Journal of Community Justice 5*, 1, 19–42.

Beckett, R., Beech, A., Fisher, D. and Fordum, A. (1994) *Community-Based Treatment for Sex Offenders: An Evaluation of Seven Treatment Programmes.* London: Home Office.

Beech, A., Erickson, M., Friendship, C. and Ditchfield, J. (2001) A *Six-Year Follow-up of Men Going Through Probation-Based Sex Offender Treatment Programmes.* Home Office Research Findings 144. London: Home Office.

Beech, A., Fisher, D., Beckett, R. and Scott-Fordham, A. (1998) *An Evaluation of the Prison Sex Offender.* London: Home Office.

Boyd, W. (2009) *Ordinary Thunderstorms.* London: Bloomsbury.

Briggs, D., Doyle, P., Gooch, T. and Kennington, R. (1998) *Assessing Men Who Sexually Abuse: A Practice Guide.* London: Jessica Kingsley Publishers.

Brown, R.E. and Dandurand, Y. (2007) 'Successful strategies that contribute to safer communities.' Paper presented to the 16th United Nations Commission on Crime Prevention and Criminal Justice in Vienna. Vancouver, Canada: International Centre for Criminal Law Reform and Criminal Justice Policy.

Bunting, L. (2005) *Females who Sexually Offend against Children: Responses of the Child Protection and Criminal Justice Systems.* London: NSPCC.

Carich, M., Wilson, C., Carich, P. and Calder, M. (2010) 'Contemporary Sex Offender Treatment: Incorporating Circles of Support and the Good Lives Model.' In J. Brayford, F. Cowe and J. Deering (eds) *What Else Works? Creative Work with Offenders.* Cullompton: Willan Publishing.

Channel 4 (2007) *Secret Life.*

Chiet, R.E. (2003) 'What hysteria? A systematic study of newspaper coverage of accused child molesters.' *Child Abuse & Neglect 27*, 607–623.

ChildLine (2003) *Annual Report.* London: ChildLine.

Circles UK (2009) Circles UK Code of Practice Version 2, March 2009.

Cohen, S. (1972) *Folk Devils and Moral Panics. The Creation of Mods and Rockers.* London: MacGibbon and Kee.

Cohen, S. (2002) *Folk Devils and Moral Panics. The Creation of Mods and Rockers.* Abingdon: Routledge. Third edition.

Cole, D. (2003) *Enemy Aliens: Double Standards and Constitutional Freedoms in the War on Terrorism.* New York, NY: The New Press.

Cossins, A. (2000) 'Masculinities, sexualities and child sexual abuse.' In G. Mair and R. Tarling (eds). Papers from the British Society of Criminology Conference, Liverpool 1999. *British Society of Criminology,* June 2000.

Criminal Justice Joint Inspection (2010) 'Restriction and Rehabilitation: Getting the Right Mix.' *An Inspection of the Management of Sexual Offenders in the Community.* Manchester: Criminal Justice Joint Inspection.

Critcher, C. (2002) 'Media, government and moral panic: The politics of paedophilia in Britain.' *Journalism Studies 3,* 4, 521–535.

Cross, S. (2005) 'Paedophiles in the community: Inter-agency conflict, news leaks and the local press.' *Crime, Media and Culture 1,* 284–300.

Cullen, F.T. (2002) 'Rehabilitation and Treatment Programmes.' In J.Q. Wilson and J. Petersilia (eds) *Crime: Public Policies for Crime Control.* Oakland, CA: Institute for Contemporary Studies.

Davidson, J.C. (2008) *Child Sexual Abuse: Media Representations and Government Reactions.* Abingdon: Routledge-Cavendish.

Devon and Cornwall Multi-Agency Public Protection Arrangements (2010) *Annual Report 2009–10.*

Eldridge, H. (1998) *The Therapist's Guide for Maintaining Change: Relapse Prevention for Adult Male Perpetrators of Child Sexual Abuse.* London: Sage.

Finkelhor, D. (1984) *Child Sexual Abuse: New Theory and Research.* New York, NY: Free Press

Ford, H. and Beech, A. (2004a) *An Assessment of the Need for Residential Treatment Facilities for Child Sexual Offenders.* London: National Probation Service for England and Wales.

Ford, H. and Beech, A. (2004b) *The Effectiveness of the Wolvercote Clinic Residential Treatment Programme in Producing Short-Term Treatment Changes and Reducing Sexual Reconvictions.* London: National Probation Service for England and Wales.

Glaser, B. (2010) 'Sex offender programmes: New technology coping with old ethics.' *Journal of Sexual Aggression 16,* 3, 264–274.

Glasser, M., Kolvin, I., Campbell, D., Glasser, A., Leitch, I. and Farrelly, S. (2001) 'Cycle of child sexual abuse: Links between the victims and becoming a perpetrator.' *British Journal of Psychiatry 179,* 482–494.

Greer, C. (2003) *Sex Crime and the Media: Sex Offending and the Press in a Divided Society.* Cullompton: Willan Publishing.

Grubin, D. (1998) *Sex Offending against Children: Understanding the Risk.* Police Research Series, Paper 99. London: Home Office.

Hanson, R.K., Gordon, A., Marques, J.K., Murphy, W. and Quinsey, V.I. (2002) 'First report of the collaborative outcome data project on the effectiveness of psychological treatment for sex offenders.' *Sexual Abuse: Journal of Research and Treatment 14*, 2, 169–194.

Hanson, R.K. and Thornton, D. (2000) 'Improving risk assessment for sexual offenders: A comparison of three actuarial scales.' *Law and Human Behaviour 24*, 119–136.

HM Prison Service (2002) *Offender Assessment System User. Version 2.* London: Home Office.

Johnson, B. (2008) 'Paedophiles face curbs on internet use.' *The Guardian*, 4 April 2008.

Jupp, V. (1989) *Methods of Criminological Research.* London: Routledge.

Kemshall, H. (2003) *Understanding Risk in Criminal Justice.* Maidenhead: Open University Press.

Kennington, R. (2008) Private communication to T. Philpot.

Kilroy-Silk, R. (2002) 'What a waste of our cash.' *Sunday Express*, 1 September 2002.

Kitzinger, J. (1996) 'Media representation of sexual abuse risks.' *Child Abuse Review 5*, 319–333.

Kitzinger, J. (2004) *Framing Abuse: Media Influence and Public Understanding of Sexual Violence Against Children.* London: Pluto Press.

Kitzinger, J. and Skidmore, P. (1995) 'Playing safe: Media coverage of child sexual abuse prevention strategies.' *Child Abuse Review 4*, 47–56.

Lovell, E. (2002) *'I Think I Might Need Some More Help with This Problem.'* London: NSPCC.

McAlinden, A. (2010) 'Restorative Justice and the Reintegration of High-Risk Sex Offenders.' In K. Harrison (ed.) *Managing High-Risk Sex Offenders in the Community.* Cullompton: Willan Publishing.

McCartney, J. (2000) 'The mob rules, OK.' *Daily Telegraph*, 13 August 2000.

McGuire, J. (1995) *What Works: Reducing Re-offending: Guidelines from Research and Practice.* Chichester: John Wiley.

Mann, R.E. and Hollin, C.R. (2007) 'Sexual offenders' explanations for their offending.' *Journal of Sexual Aggression 13*, 1, 3–9.

Mann, R.E., O'Brien, M., Thornton, D., Rallings, M. and Webster, S. (2002) *Structured Assessment of Risk and Need.* London: HM Prison Department.

Mann, R. and Shingler, J. (2006) 'Collaboration in Clinical Work with Sex Offenders: Treatment and Risk Assessment.' In W.L. Marshall, Y.E. Fernandez, L.E. Marshall and G.A. Serran (eds) *Sexual Offender Treatment: Controversial Issues.* Chichester: John Wiley.

Mann, R. and Thornton, D. (1998) 'The Evolution of a Multisite Sexual Offender Treatment Programme.' In W. Marshall, Y. Fernandez, S. Hudson and T. Ward (eds) *Sourcebook of Treatment Programs for Sexual Offenders.* New York, NY: Plenum Press.

Marshall, P. (1997) *The Prevalence of Convictions for Sexual Offending: Research Findings No. 55.* London: Home Office.

Marshall, W.L., Barbaree, H.E. and Fernandez, Y.M. (1999) *Cognitive Behavioural Treatment of Sexual Offenders.* Chichester: John Wiley.

Marshall, W.L., Fernandez, Y.M., Serran, G.A., Mulloy, R. *et al.* (2003) 'Process variables in the treatment of sex offenders. A review of the relevant literature.' *Journal of Aggression and Violent Behaviour 8*, 205–234.

Milmo, C. (2000a) 'Mob rule in Portsmouth: Police offer to help those indicted by rumour.' *The Independent*, 10 August 2000.

Milmo, C. (2000b) 'Unashamed lynch law simmers on rundown estate.' *The Independent*, 9 August 2000.

Moran, C. (2010) 'Do "special" and "daddy" imply menace?' *Sunday Times*, 17 April 2010.

Nellis, M. (2008) 'Circles of Support and Accountability for sex offenders in England and Wales: Their origins and implementation 1999–2005.' *British Journal of Community Justice 7*, 23–44.

Niechcial, J. (2010) *Lucy Faithfull: Mother to Hundreds*. Privately published.

Parris, M. (1997) 'All-party witch hunt.' *The Times*, 24 January 1997.

Philpot, T. (2009) *Understanding Child Abuse: The Partners of Child Sex Offenders Tell Their Stories*. London: Routledge.

Prescott, D. and Levenson, J. (2010). 'Sex offender treatment is not punishment.' *Journal of Sexual Aggression 16*, 3, 275–285.

Proulex, J., Tardif, M., Lamoureux, B. and Lussier, P. (2000) 'How Does Recidivism Risk Assessment Predict Survival?' In D.R. Laws, S.M. Hudson and T. Ward (eds) *Remaking Relapse Prevention with Sex Offenders*. London: Sage Publications.

Quaker Peace and Social Witness (2005) *Circles of Support and Accountability in the Thames Valley: The First Three Years – April 2002 to March 2005*. London: Quaker Communications.

Salter, A. (2003) *Predators, Paedophiles, Rapists and Other Sex Offenders: Who They Are, How They Operate and How We Can Protect Ourselves and Our Children*. New York, NY: Basic Books.

Sanderson, C. (2004) *The Seduction of Children: Empowering Parents and Teachers to Protect Children from Sexual Abuse*. London: Jessica Kingsley Publishers.

Saunders, R. and Wilson, C. (2003) 'Circles of Support and Accountability in the Thames Valley: Questions and answers.' *NOTA News 45*, July 2003.

Silverman, J. and Wilson, D. (2002) *Innocence Betrayed: Paedophilia, the Media and Society*. Cambridge: Polity Press.

Skuse, D. (2003) Quoted in *The Guardian* and in Sanderson, C. (2004) *The Seduction of Children: Empowering Parents and Teachers to Protect Children from Sexual Abuse*. London: Jessica Kingsley Publishers.

Stuart, M. and Baines, C. (2004) *Safeguards for Vulnerable Children: Three Studies on Abusers, Disabled Children and Children in Prison*. York: Joseph Rowntree Foundation.

Thomas, T. (2010) 'The Sex Offender Register, Community Notification and Some Reflections on Privacy.' In Harrison, K. (ed.) *Managing High-Risk Sex Offenders in the Community*. Cullompton: Willan Publishing.

Walker, A., Kershaw, C. and Nicholas, S. (2004) *Crime in England and Wales 2005–6*. London: Home Office.

Walsh, P. (no date) 'Therapeutic strategies for sex offenders: Contents and rationale.' Unpublished paper.

Ward, T. and Maruna, S. (2007) *Rehabilitation*. London: Routledge.

Ward, T. and Stewart, C. (2003) 'Criminogenic needs and human needs: A theoretical model.' *Psychology, Crime and Law 9*, 125–143.

Wilson, C., Bates, A. and Völlm, B. (2010) 'Circles of Support and Accountability: An innovative approach to manage high-risk sex offenders in the community.' *The Open Criminology Journal 3/2010*, 48–57.

Wilson, R., Cortoni, F. and McWhinnie, A. (2009) *Circles of Support and Accountability: A Canadian National Replication of Outcome Findings.* London: Sage.

Wilson, R.J., McWhinnie, A.J., Picheca, J.E., Prinzo, M. and Cortoni, F. (2007a) 'Circles of Support and Accountability: Engaging community volunteers in the management of high-risk sexual offenders. Part 1: Effects on participants and stakeholders.' *Howard Journal of Criminal Justice 46*, 289–302.

Wilson, R.J., McWhinnie, A.J., Picheca, J.E. and Prinzo, M. (2007b) 'Evaluating the effectiveness of professionally facilitated volunteerism in the community-based management of high-risk sexual offenders. Part 2: Recidivism rates.' *Howard Journal of Criminal Justice 46*, 327–337.

Wilson, R., McWhinnie, A. and Wilson, C. (2008) 'Circles of Support and Accountability: An international partnership in reducing sexual offender recidivism.' *Prison Service Journal 178*, 26–36.

Wilson, R.J., Picheca, J.E. and Prinzo, M. (2005) *Circles of Support and Accountability: An Evaluation of the Pilot Project in South-Central Ontario.* Research Report R.168. Ottawa ON: Correctional Service of Canada.

Wolf, S.C. (1984) 'A multifactor model of deviant sexuality.' Paper presented at the Third International Conference on Victimology, Lisbon, Portugal, November 1984. Quoted in Sanderson, C. (2004) *The Seduction of Children: Empowering Parents and Teachers to Protect Children from Sexual Abuse.* London: Jessica Kingsley Publishers.

Wood, J. and Kemshall, H. (2010) Effective Multi-Agency Public Protection: Learning from the Research.' In K. Harrison (ed.) *Managing High-Risk Sex Offenders in the Community.* Cullompton: Willan Publishing.

Wyre, R. (2007) Talk on the partners of sex offenders. *Community Care Live*, London, 11 October 2007.

About the Authors

Stephen Hanvey is the first chief executive of Circles UK. He has held managerial posts in a number of voluntary agencies, including Victim Support and Barnardo's, where he established a community development project in east London. He has worked voluntarily as a group facilitator with survivors of sexual abuse. With a professional background in social work and child care, he also holds a Diploma in Executive Coaching and Organisational Development.

Terry Philpot is a journalist and writer. He writes occasionally for *The Tablet*, *The Guardian* and other publications. He has written, co-written and edited more than a dozen books on subjects ranging from adoption to learning disability. His last book was *Understanding Child Abuse: The Female Partners of Sex Offenders Tell Their Stories* (Routledge 2009). He has also published two reports on residential services run by religious orders and on kinship care and private fostering. He is a volunteer for New Bridge, which works with prisoners, and a mentor with the Cardinal Hume Centre of which he is also a trustee. He is also a trustee of the Centre for Policy on Ageing.

Chris Wilson, who qualified as a social worker in 1983, is national development manager for Circles UK. He joined the Probation Service in 1992 working in the field of sexual aggression. He was appointed in 2002 as project manager for Hampshire and Thames Valley Circles of Support and Accountability, and was instrumental in adapting the Canadian Circles model to a British context. Formerly treatment manager at the Thames Valley Sex Offender Project, he was a member of the design team for the accredited Thames Valley Sex Offender Group work programme. He has contributed to the book *What Else Works? Creative Work with Offenders* (Willan Press 2010) and has written and co-written numerous articles on Circles for professional journals.

Subject Index

Author Index